M. Keith Williams

The Godly Woman
Teacher's Guide

Irma Warr
Foreword by Charlie Riggs

M. Keith Williams

Creative Resources

Waco, Texas

Teacher's Guide
THE GODLY WOMAN

Copyright ©1976 by The Warr Foundation, Oklahoma City, Oklahoma 73132

Printed in the United States of America.

When Scripture references are from versions other than the King James version, they are designated as follows:
LB—Living Bible
RSV—Revised Standard Version
AMP—Amplified
NASB—New American Standard Bible
Phillips—Phillips

Special acknowledgement to the Navigators for permission to use their material in much of the Appendix, and to my husband, Gene, who wrote the "Bible Discussion Group Leader's Manual" contained in the Appendix.

Library of Congress Catalog Card Number: 76-40602

Acknowledgements

My Special Thanks

—To my husband, Gene, who did *so much* of the research work
and constantly counseled and encouraged me along the way . . .
and whose love keeps me going.

—To my three sons—my treasures—Kevin, Kyle, and Kory who·
often gave me those "diversions" every writer *needs* in the
middle of a thought (to make a peanut butter sandwich, or change
a diaper, or hear a story, or kiss a hurt)! . . . and without whom
the chapters on being a mother could not have been written.

—To those who have typed and proofread the manuscripts, and the
girls who helped in our home to allow me to have time to write.

—To the men in my husband's Bible Study who did so much of the
original research work and helped greatly by prayer.

—To the girls in my Bible Study who helped so much through
prayer, research, encouragement, checking and proofreading
manuscripts, etc.

Contents

Foreword
A Message to the Teacher
About the Material

The Godly Woman as a Disciple

The Godly Woman as Christ's Representative

The Godly Woman as a Wife

The Godly Woman as a Mother

Foreword

Today, perhaps more than at any time in history, multitudes are meeting together in small Bible study and prayer fellowship groups. A tremendous spiritual hunger is being met by a variety of good study material that are currently available.

Personally, I believe that *The Godly* Woman study is unique. To begin with, in the *Personal Bible Studies* workbook, you have an excellent combination of well designed lessons with relevance to the issues and problems of the day, deeply rooted in Scripture with practical application of biblical truth to specific areas of life. The *Teacher's Guide* is filled with a large variety of rich resource material for the leader—material that will give any teacher who does her homework great confidence in leading her group.

Another unique feature of these studies is a "built in" fellowship through prayer and sharing. Group members pray for each other daily, and in weekly Bible discussion share their Bible discoveries and what God is doing in their lives.

I am confident that any person who is willing to follow the disciplines set forth in these studies will greatly enhance her relationship to God and man and her effectiveness as a Christian witness.

Charlie Riggs
Counselor Training and Followup
The Billy Graham Evangelistic
Association

A Message to the Teacher

As the teacher, your primary purpose is to help each group member, including yourself, to develop and grow toward her unique potential as a child of God. The ultimate success of the group depends on your dedication. Therefore, try to be genuinely open in your participation and prepare the structure and mechanical details as thoroughly as possible in advance. It will be your job to lead out in all discussions. You are the catalyst.

This Teacher's Guide is not meant to be an exhaustive or comprehensive coverage of each chapter, nor does it seek to provide "perfect" answers for each of the questions in the class member workbook. Its primary purpose is to provide some helps and ideas to supplement your own preparation—not take the place of it.

Here are some suggestions for you to follow during your preparation for group meetings:

1. See that each member has a copy of *The Godly Woman: Personal Bible Studies for the Christian Woman*. This is their "workbook" and should be brought to every class meeting.
2. Familiarize yourself with the printed material in both your Teacher's Guide and in the *Personal Bible Studies* workbook. Note the similarities and differences between the two.
3. Before you begin the course, read and study the "Bible Discussion Group Leader's Manual" found in the Appendix to this book (p.133). No one can realistically follow all the suggestions found there, and you certainly don't have to know it all to have an effective group experience. It is simply offered to stimulate your thinking, make the class more effective, and to be a reference source for those who desire to accept the responsibility of leading a Bible discussion group.
4. Before the meeting time, listen completely to the audio

cassette portions recommended for each session. There will be two listening assignments for each meeting: (1) a segment for you, the teacher, and (2) a portion for the group to hear during the last ten minutes of the class meeting.

5. As you use the tapes, notice that a narrator clearly identifies each chapter immediately prior to the actual listening segment.

6. Following the listening segment, your cue to turn the recorder off will be a 10-second pause.

7. Make sure the audio cassettes are clear, audible, and otherwise free from manufacturing defects. In the event of any problems, don't hesitate to return defective cassettes to Word, Inc. shipping offices at 100 Publishers Drive, Winona Lake, Indiana 46590, and request an immediate replacement.

The Godly Woman study course has a companion program entitled *The Godly Man*. They are similar in design and format. This enables couples to participate in the same class together. If used in this way, we suggest the following:

1. Couples can be combined except on those specific sessions which apply only to men or to women (session nine, sessions sixteen through twenty, and session twenty-two).

2. For these sessions, divide the two groups and arrange to have a lady lead the women's study.

3. The men will need a copy of *The Godly Man: Personal Bible Studies for the Christian Man* workbook, and women a copy of *The Godly Woman: Personal Bible Studies for the Christian Woman* workbook.

4. When leading the combined sessions, the teacher should be aware of the differences between the material for *The Godly Man* study and the material for *The Godly Woman* study (e.g. the photographs contained only in the men's workbook; and the Teacher's Guides references to pages in the men's and women's workbook).

5. These differences also pertain to the cassette tapes which are to be used during the last 10 minutes of each session. At this point, the groups should be divided so each one can hear their respective audio presentation.

6. You will need both Leader's Kits (*The Godly Man* and *The Godly Woman*) when conducting combined couples sessions.

Remember, the privilege of leading women in discovering the truths and treasures of the Bible is a sacred responsibility which deserves—and necessitates—your prayerful preparation and total dependence and yieldedness to the Holy Spirit.

About the Material

Purpose
To challenge people to take the Christian faith seriously and to help them grow up to a fuller maturity in Christ.

Setting
This course is designed for any of the following groups:

1. Sunday school classes
2. Home study groups
3. Study courses
4. Elective religion courses
5. Retreat sessions
6. College groups
7. Couples groups
8. Intergeneration groups
9. Bible study groups
10. Special-interest groups

Design
The complete program utilizes a Teacher's Guide, Personal Bible Studies workbook, and four tapes.

1. The Teacher's Guide is divided into seventeen chapters and an appendix. The entire course is designed for 22 sessions. (Note: Chapter III is covered in three sessions and Chapter XV in four.) Each session is divided into basically six divisions: (A) Object of the lesson; (B) Discussion questions; (C) Additional scriptures; (E) Possible projects; (F) Extra helps (books, studies, or tapes to recommend). You will find this probably provides for more material than you can cover and

that some of it is not pertinent to your group. You will need to be selective and choose the questions, project, etc., which you feel will be most helpful to your group. The books and pamphlets mentioned in the "Extra Helps" may be obtained from your local Christian bookstore. The tapes are available on a free loan basis from:

The Foundation Library
435 West Boyd
Norman, Oklahoma 73069

2. The *Personal Bible Studies for the Christian Woman* notebook has been prepared so it can be used by a group of women or by individuals for personal study. It is meant to be written in. When used in group setting, each woman should complete all the activities for that chapter *prior* to the meeting time and bring her workbook to the group meeting.

3. There are four 90-minute tapes in the leader's kit. Two tapes are for the teacher's preparation and two tapes are to be used during the class meeting. For each session there is one listening segment for the teacher to listen to prior to the meeting, and one listening segment for the group to be played during the last few minutes of the class period.

Scheduling

The Godly Woman study can be used with a variety of scheduling plans:

1. STUDY GROUP PLAN—This plan is designed for groups meeting on a regular basis in neighborhood homes. You would meet once a week for eleven 1½-2 hour meetings, covering two sessions per meeting.

2. SUNDAY SCHOOL PLAN—This plan is designed for groups meeting weekly during the regular Sunday morning teaching period. You would meet once a week for twenty-two, 1 hour sessions following the regular outline given in the table of contents.

3. RETREAT PLAN—This plan is designed for a retreat setting where a Friday evening, all day Saturday, and Sunday morning are available. Advance publicity should clarify the theme

and purpose of the retreat. The *Personal Bible Studies* workbook should be distributed at least ten days prior to retreat time, and all outside preparation should be completed before the conference. Obviously, time would not permit covering twenty-two sessions. Possibly ten might be the most that could be reasonably completed. The teacher should use her own creativity and planning at this point. You may want to select one question from each session, or select only those sessions which would most interest your particular group.

4. STUDY COURSE PLAN—This plan is designed for a Sunday-to-Friday (evenings) conference of six, 2-hour sessions. Advance preparation is necessary. As in the retreat plan, you may have to be selective in your use of the material.

Advance Planning

You may want to take into account several suggestions as you plan to use this material:

1. RECOMMENDING THE COURSE—If you are selecting or recommending this course to a group leader (such as church staff member, department superintendent, committee chairman) meet personally with the group leader or teacher. Review the material thoroughly. If interest is shown, discuss and consider possibilities. Decide together how best to use the materials in a way which the group leader feels good about—assuring him that the tapes and written materials handle the difficult transitions.

2. SELECTING THE COURSE—If you are a group leader or teacher, you probably have secured the initial *The Godly Woman* kit as possible resource material. At your regular group meeting, display the material. Spend time reviewing and evaluating. If your group is the responsibility of your church (Sunday school, etc.) be sure to meet with your educational director, curriculum committee, or pastor for further discussion on how best to adapt the course for your use.

3. FINANCING THE COURSE—It is recommended that enrollment be taken each time the course is offered. Everyone who enrolls in the course must have a *The Godly Woman: Personal Bible Studies for the Christian Woman* workbook

($2.95). If your church is not in a position to purchase all or part of the materials, an enrollment fee will be necessary. Conference, convention, and workshop experience has proven that attendance, participation, and personal benefit are increased when a registration fee is required. Depending on the total enrollment, $5.00 per person will usually cover each one's workbook and the initial *The Godly Woman* kit which includes the leader's materials. Remember, no matter how much planning is done, this course will probably not work unless the participants are motivated. As the teacher, your sensitivity at this point is essential.

4. ORDERING MATERIALS—You may order additional *The Godly Woman: Personal Bible Studies for the Christian Woman* workbooks (Cat. #40123), Teacher's Guides (Cat. #40122) and Teacher's Kits (Cat. #CRC–0642) from your local bookstore, or write directly to Creative Resources, P.O. Box 1790, Waco, Texas, 76703, or call toll free 1–800–433-2380. When ordering, please use the catalog number given above and allow four to six weeks for shipping and handling.

5. FOLLOW-UP—*The Godly Woman* is one of several study courses which are similar in design and format. For a complete description of these and over fifty additional group study programs available through Creative Resources, write/call P.O. Box 1790, Waco, Texas, 76703, 1–800–433-2380. A no-obligation thirty-day review program is available on all cassette resources ordered through a service representative of the Telephone Marketing Division.

6. LEADERSHIP TRAINING—Every member who completes this course has, as a result, received some indirect training in group process and leadership skills. Because the tapes and Leader's Guide handle the difficult transitions and provide detailed instructions, each participant becomes a potential group leader. Following the last session, if you decide not to continue with the same group, encourage the participants to secure a *The Godly Woman* Teacher's Kit and start their own study group.

CHAPTER I
THE FOUNDATION OF A DISCIPLE

The Bible says, "for other foundation can no man lay than that is laid, which is Jesus Christ." (I Corinthians 3:11). We are very aware that the Biblical principles set forth in the Godly Woman will not be received nor personally applied unless the women doing the study know Jesus Christ as their personal Savior and Lord. Being a Christian is the *necessary* and *only* foundation for being a disciple. So we urge you to prayerfully prepare for Lesson 1 and ask God to enable you to "know the state of your flocks." Proverbs 27:23.

A. *OBJECT OF THE LESSON*

1. To make sure all in the class know Jesus Christ as Savior and have assurance that they have eternal life.

2. To make sure everyone has a clear understanding of the gospel and can clearly and simply present it to another.

B. *DISCUSSION QUESTIONS*

Probably the women taking this course are already Christians; that is, they have made the wonderful discovery of knowing Christ personally. However, we do not want to take anything for granted. So it would be well if you would take a few minutes at the beginning of this first class and say something like this to your class:
"The Godly Woman Study was written for Christian women and therefore, I think it would be fitting to begin our study today by asking:

1. What in your opinion is a Christian?

2. How does one become a Christian? (question 18 in their book)

3. If you answered question 19 in your book with a "yes", would you share how you KNOW you have eternal life?

The discussion of these three questions by the class, as well as your comments, should provide a clear presentation of the Gospel for any non-Christians in the group. And if all in the class do happen to be Christians, this will be a good exercise for them in learning to articulate clearly and simply the Gospel message. Also, quite often there are those who *have* accepted Jesus Christ as their Savior, but have no assurance of salvation. These people sometimes find it difficult to express these doubts. It would be worthwhile to have the ladies look up the following verses and share the basis of assurance they find in each one: Romans 10:13; Romans 10:9; John 3:16; John 5:24; John 3:36; I Jn. 5:12,13.

Teacher, be especially prayerful and careful how you (or anyone else in the class) responds if one of the ladies obviously has the wrong answers to these questions or does not clearly understand what it means to be a Christian. You might say, "Let's look again at God's Word and see what He says." Then take them through the Steps to Peace With God (which is included in the Godly Woman Bible Study book and also in the Teacher's Guide) or perhaps you would prefer to make an appointment with the person when you could discuss it with her individually.

OTHER POSSIBLE QUESTIONS

1. What divine attribute of Jesus means the most to you? (e.g. His authority? His love? His acceptance? His forgiveness? That He is personal? Real? Alive? etc.) Why?

2. What human characteristic of Jesus means the most to you (e.g. that He was tempted, yet was sinless? His suffering? His commonness?) Why? (Heb. 4:15; Heb. 2:14. He knows what it's like to be *me*. . . . and no banqueting in heaven or angel bands or celestial music will ever make Him forget what it's like to be *me,—you,—human*. (See "What is God Like", by Eugenia Price, Chapter 8)

3. What did Jesus have to do with creation? (John 1:1-3; Heb. 1:1-2)

What does He have to do with the operating of the natural laws today? (Col. 1:16)

4. What does Luke 19:10 mean to you? How does He seek? How does He save? Is conversion the completion of salvation? Explain.
(It's the beginning, like crossing the threshold. Beyond conversion there is a life time of growing in the grace and knowledge of Jesus, as Peter pointed out in II Peter 3:18.)

5. Share Romans 6:23 in your own words.

6. Why is the resurrection important to genuine Christianity? I Cor. 15:13-20. (Christianity is the only religion of the world that has a living leader. If Jesus Christ did not come forth from the tomb, then He is not who He claimed to be and Christianity is a farce.)

7. How many people does God want saved? (I Tim. 2:4; II Pet. 3:9)
How many people will be? Why? (Mt. 7:13,14)

8. What are some of the reasons why some people don't become Christians? (Lack of faith, have never seen a live demonstration of Christ in a life, Satan has blinded them, don't know how, don't want to change, pride, the world's influence, they have a quiet, dignified love for sin.)

9. What is repentence? (Mt. 3:2, In Wuest is translated "Be having a change of mind which issues in a change of conduct." Verse 8 says "Produce fruit therefore weighing as much as the repentence you profess.")
How important is repentence in conversion? Why? (Luke 13:3,5)

(Without repentence there can be no conversion. It is more than simply being sorry for our sins. It is a change of mind about God, about sin, about ourselves, It inevitably produces a change of life's direction.)

C. SUGGESTIONS FOR CONCLUSION

Teacher, here are some possible ways you might conclude this lesson.

1. Ask the group to look back through the lesson and choose something about God or Christ they are especially thankful for today. Ask several to offer a prayer of thanks (out loud) for that one particular thing.

2. Read "My Advocate".

MY ADVOCATE

By Martha Snell Nicholson

I sinned. And straightway, post-haste, Satan flew
Before the presence of the most high God,
And made a railing accusation there.
He said, "This soul, this thing of clay and sod,
Has sinned. 'Tis true that he has named Thy name
But I demand his death, for Thou hast said,
"The soul that sinneth it shall die". Shall not
Thy sentence be fulfilled? Is justice dead?
Send now this wretched sinner to his doom.
What other thing can righteous ruler do?"
And thus he did accuse me day and night,
And every word he spoke, O God, was true!

Then quickly One rose up from God's right hand,
Before Whose glory angels veiled their eyes.
He spoke, "Each jot and tittle of the law
Must be fulfilled; the guilty sinner dies!
But wait—suppose his guilt were all transferred
to ME, and that I paid his penalty!
Behold My hands, My side, My feet! One day
I was made sin for him, and died that he
Might be presented, faultless, at Thy throne!"
And Satan flew away. Full well he knew
That he could not prevail against such love,
For every word my dear Lord spoke was true.

3. Say: "Let's close today by bowing our heads and silently answering these three questions: (1) Do you know, beyond any shadow of a doubt that you are a Christian? (2) Do you know how to share with another the good news of how one becomes a Christian? (3) Will you prayerfully seek to share this good news with someone this week?"
Close with prayer.

D. *ADDITIONAL SCRIPTURES*

John 5:24; 6:37; 10:28; II Tim. 2:13 (LB); I Pet. 1:3,4

E. *POSSIBLE PROJECTS*

1. Write out and share their testimony.

2. Answer: "If you should find yourself at heaven's door and Gabriel asked you, 'What right do you have to be here?' exactly what would you say?"

3. Memorize I Jn. 5:11,12 or I Pet. 2:24 and share it.

4. Give each class member a different booklet (from the ones listed under Extra Helps) and ask each one to give a report the following week.

F. *EXTRA HELPS*

Here's How published by Life Messengers
Is Christianity Credible, Moody Press
My Heart, Christ's Home, Billy Graham Evangelistic Association
The Reason Why, Moody Press
Know Why You Believe by Paul Little, Victor Books
How to Give Away Your Faith, InterVarsity Press
Evidence That Demands a Verdict by Josh McDowell, Campus Crusade for Christ, Inc.

CHAPTER II
GOD'S PROVISION FOR A DISCIPLE

Grace, amazing grace . . . *This* is God's provision for a disciple. Writers down through the ages have tried to describe and illustrate the preciousness of God's grace to the believer. Listen to these words:

Wonderful Grace of Jesus

Wonderful grace of Jesus, greater than all my sin;
How shall my tongue describe it, where shall its praise begin?
Taking away my burden, setting my spirit free;
For the wonderful grace of Jesus reaches me.

Wonderful grace of Jesus, reaching to all the lost,
By it I have been pardoned, saved to the uttermost.
Chains have been torn asunder, giving me liberty;
For the wonderful grace of Jesus reaches me.

Wonderful grace of Jesus, reaching the most defiled,
By its transforming power, making him God's dear child,
Purchasing peace and heaven, for all eternity;
And the wonderful grace of Jesus reaches me.

Wonderful the matchless grace of Jesus,
Deeper than the mighty rolling sea;
Higher than the mountain, sparkling like a fountain,
All sufficient grace for even me.
Broader than the scope of my transgressions,
Greater far than all my sin and shame;
O magnify the precious name of Jesus, Praise His name!

Haldor Lillenas

Amazing Grace! How Sweet the Sound

Amazing grace! how sweet the sound that saved a wretch like
    me!
I once was lost, but now am found, Was blind, but now I see.

'Twas grace that taught my heart to fear, and grace my fears
    relieved;
How precious did that grace appear the hour I first believed!

Through many dangers, toils and snares, I have already come;
'Tis grace hath brought me safe thus far, and grace will lead
me home.

When we've been there ten thousand years, bright shining as
    the sun,
We've no less days to sing God's praise than when we first begun.

John Newton

Grace Greater than Our Sin

Marvelous grace of our loving Lord, grace that exceeds our sin
    and our guilt,
Yonder on Calvary's mount outpoured, there where the blood
    of the Lamb was spilt.

Sin and despair like the sea waves cold, threaten the soul with
    infinite loss;
Grace that is greater, yes, grace untold, points to the Refuge,
    the mighty Cross.

Dark is the stain that we cannot hide, what can avail to wash
    it away?
Look! there is flowing a crimson tide; whiter than snow you may
    be today.

Marvelous, infinite, matchless grace, freely bestowed on all
    who believe;
You that are longing to see His face, will you this moment
    His grace receive?

Julia H. Johnston

Grace, grace—God's grace,
Grace that will pardon and cleanse within;
Grace, grace, God's grace,
Grace that is greater than all our sin.

Teacher, perhaps you would like to start your class today by reading these words to the class. Or, if possible, provide a copy of the words for each one to have. Then ask the ladies to thank God for some particular aspect of grace mentioned in these songs. You might want to have sentence prayers, inviting each one to pray several times as they meditate on the various facets of God's grace.

A. *OBJECT OF THE LESSON*

1. To identify God's grace as the means of salvation and growth and know how to appropriate it.

2. To recognize the grace of God, properly appreciate it, and respond in love because of it.

B. *DISCUSSION QUESTIONS*

1. In what specific way have you experienced the grace of God?

2. What does the phrase "My grace is sufficient for you" (II Cor. 12:9) mean to you? (Teacher, have them read it in several translations. Note: the Lord says "My grace *IS* sufficient"—that means *now*, present tense, at the point of need!)

3. What does it mean to "frustrate" the grace of God? (to receive grace but not be gracious; to continue to look at things from your own point of view; to remain a spiritual babe; to not share His grace with others.)

4. In Col. 2:9,10, what does the word, "complete" mean? (The Living Bible says "So you have everything when you have Christ") Is *complete* the same as *mature*? (No—A baby is complete—but not mature. The same is true spiritually. At conversion we are complete in Christ, but we must grow to maturity.)

5. What does "everything" in I Cor. 1:4,5 include?

—8—

6. What are some areas of self-effort in your life? Which of these are you going to allow God to work on this week? (#14)

7. Look at I Peter 4:10. What do we learn about grace in this verse? (not given for selfish use. The Living Bible gives a good paraphrase.)

8. What does II Cor. 6:1 mean when it says "receive not the grace of God in vain"?

9. Share your application on page 10. (questions 18 and 19).

C. *SUGGESTIONS FOR CONCLUSION*

Teacher, look back at the object of today's lesson. Have you accomplished it? Perhaps you might close your class today along these lines.

"How much grace do you think you can count on receiving from God? (Romans 5:20). Annie Johnson Flint in her poem "He Giveth More," shows us how limitless is the supply of grace available.

He Giveth More

He giveth more grace when the burdens grow greater,
  He sendeth more strength when the labors increase;
To added affliction He addeth His mercy,
  To multiplied trials, His multiplied peace.

When we have exhausted our store of endurance,
  When our strength has failed ere the day is half done,
When we reach the end of our hoarded resources,
  Our Father's full giving is only begun.

He love has no limit, His grace has no measure,
  His power no boundary known unto men;
For out of His infinite riches in Jesus
  He giveth and giveth and giveth again.

* * * *

An old college professor at a Christian college often said to his students: "Young people, if it's grace you need, help yourself. There's plenty of it!"

"What is it you need grace for today? Will you 'help yourself' and then thank Him for His provision as we close in prayer."

D. *ADDITIONAL SCRIPTURES*

Romans 12:2, Phil. 4:19, I Cor. 4:7, II Pet. 3:18

E. *POSSIBLE PROJECTS*

1. Write down the one thing worrying you most today. Pray daily during the coming week for God to reveal how his grace is sufficient for that one thing.

2. Make a list of good things that have come your way and evaluate whether they came by your efforts or by God's grace. II Cor. 9:8.

3. During the coming week, list the times when you depend on God's grace and be prepared to share those with the group.

4. List the times when you have been most afraid and what you did about it?

5. Memorize a verse pertinent to this lesson and share it with the group.

F. *EXTRA HELPS*

The Taste of New Wine by Keith Miller
Victory in Christ by Trumbell
The Normal Christian Life by Watchman Nee
The Latent Power of the Soul by Nee
The Christian's Secret to a Happy Life by H. W. Smith
Grace by F. S. Schaeffer
Keys to Triumphant Living by Taylor

CHAPTER III

THE CHRIST-CENTERED LIFE
(WHEEL ILLUSTRATION)

Chapter three is divided into three parts. These 3 parts are each meant to be studied as a separate assignment. Since they are rather short you may feel your class needs a longer assignment. If so, you may wish to assign them some of the additional questions or projects given in the Teacher's Guide for these three parts of Chapter Three. Or perhaps you will want to divide it into two lessons instead of three. (e.g. page 14-16 as one assignment and pages 17-21 as the second assignment.)

However, it would be impossible to overestimate the value of these chapters on "THE CHRIST CENTERED LIFE". So do not rush through them. Take the time necessary to be sure each one in the class grasps the necessity of Christ being the *center* of their lives and the importance of living a balanced Christian life.

PART I—The Hub and The Rim

A. *OBJECT OF THE LESSON*

    1. To present an overview of the balanced Christian life.

    2. To communicate the necessity of Christ being the very center of one's life and to show how this is achieved only through obedience to His Word.

B. *DISCUSSION QUESTIONS*
  GENERAL QUESTIONS ON THE WHEEL

    1. In what ways do you feel the Christian life is illustrated by The Wheel? (A wheel must have a hub to function. Likewise, Christ must be our hub—our center. A wheel must have all of its spokes and they must be equal to give balanced action. Likewise, the basics must be present and in balance for the Christian to be effective.)

    2. What is your opinion of the Wheel illustration?

    3. Why is nothing of the fruit of the Spirit mentioned? (Gal. 5:22,23)

4. Why are these specific four spokes used? (Because they *are the basics* of the Christian life. If these are in balance all other areas of the Christian's life will progress.)

QUESTIONS ON THE HUB—CHRIST THE CENTER

1. What is the function of the Hub of the wheel? (It furnishes the driving power and bears the weight of the wheel)

2. How does this apply to the Christian life? (Christ provides the driving power for the Christian life and bears the weight of our lives. I Peter 5:7)

3. If Christ is the center of our lives, furnishing all the driving power, how much power do we have? (Eph. 3:20,21; Col. 2:9,10; Matt. 28:18)

4. Whose responsibility is it to live the Christian life? (Christ—He alone is capable of living the Christian life. He will finish what He began in us. Phil. 1:6)

5. What then is our part? (Jn. 15:5, abiding in Him)

6. What does "abiding" mean? (Resting or staying in Him, allowing Him to live His life in and through us.)

7. Why do you think Heb. 13:8 was included as a reason for Christ being the center of our lives? Share your answer to question 2. What are other centers?

QUESTIONS ON THE RIM (OBEDIENCE)

1. In Ex. 19:5, how can we become God's peculiar treasure through obedience and still have it be grace? (obedience is the channel through which His grace comes)

2. In I Peter 1:22, explain how obedience purifies our souls.

3. Look at question 7 in your book. Name some of the sacrifices people use as substitutes for obedience.

4. Read John 14:21 again. Why is obedience so important? (proof of Lordship, proof of our love for Christ; it is best for us, and it is necessary before the Father will manifest-or make Himself known-to us).

5. In your experience, has God ever made Himself known to you as a result of obedience?

6. How did you answer number 11?

7. Why do we disobey?

8. What is the time element in obedience? (Ps. 119:59, 60)

C. SUGGESTIONS FOR CONCLUSION

Teacher, here are some possible questions to help the ladies apply the truths from this lesson:

1. What are some of the substitutions people make for Christ in the center of their lives? (Question 2, page 14)

2. Is Christ the center of your life, or have you substituted someone or something else?

3. Are you living a balanced Christian life? Do each of the four basic spokes have their rightful place in my life? If not, which areas do I need to work on?

4. What practical step can I take this week to begin to bring my life into balance as a Christian?

Have a moment of silent prayer during which you suggest that they covenant with God about *faithfully* doing this week whatever application He has brought to their minds today.

D. ADDITIONAL SCRIPTURES

Matt. 7:24-27; Gal. 2:20; Col. 1:27; Rom. 12:1,2; Luke 6:46

E. *POSSIBLE PROJECTS*

1. Draw the wheel and share it with someone this week.

2. Pick out one area of disobedience, find a verse that fits that area, and pray each day this week for victory in this area.

3. Ask God in prayer each morning to reveal areas of your life that aren't committed to Him. (Ps. 139: 23,24), then commit them to Him—particularly the one God has shown you that day.

4. Covenant to spend at least ten minutes in the Word and prayer each morning.

F. *EXTRA HELPS*

Complete in Christ by Andrew Murray
The Saving Life of Christ by Ian Thomas
We Would See Jesus by R. Hession
A Call to Commitment by Elizabeth O'Connor, Harper & Row
True Discipleship by McDonald
Tape 832—**"Christ-Centered Life."**

THE CHRIST-CENTERED LIFE
(WHEEL ILLUSTRATION)

PART II—The Vertical Intake Spokes

So many, many Christians today are still spiritual babes instead of mature Christians as they should be. They spend little or no time in the Bible and are unlearned and ignorant regarding the Word of God—and therefore know little of the *God* of the Word! They spend little time in prayer and therefore know little of the faithful, gracious God who delights in answering prayer.

We trust your class will not be in this category after studying this lesson.

Will you meditate prayerfully over the OBJECT OF THE LESSON and ask God to enable you by His Holy Spirit to communicate to these ladies the *rich* treasures that await them as they come into intimate knowledge of God and communion and fellowship with God through His Word and prayer.

Perhaps you would like to set the atmosphere for today's lesson by sharing the following:

FOUND IN EVANGELIST BILLY SUNDAY'S BIBLE

"With the Holy Spirit as my guide, I entered the wonderful temple of Christianity:

"I entered the portico of Genesis, walked down through the Old Testament art galleries, where pictures of Noah, Abraham, Moses, Joseph, Isaac, Jacob, and Daniel were hung on the walls.

"I passed into the music room of Psalms, where the Spirit swept the keyboard of nature until it seemed that every reed and pipe in God's great organ responded to the tuneful harp of David, the sweet singer of Israel.

"I entered the chamber of Ecclesiastes, where the voice of the preacher was heard; and into the conservatory of Sharon, where the Lily of the Valley's sweet scented spices filled and perfumed my life.

"I entered the business office of Proverbs, and then into the observatory room of the Prophets, where I saw telescopes of various sizes, pointed to far-off events, but all concentrated on the Bright and Morning Star.

"I entered the audience room of the King of Kings, and caught a vision of His glory from the standpoint of Matthew, Mark, Luke and John; passed into the Acts of the Apostles where the Holy Spirit was doing His work in the formation of the infant Church.

"Then into the correspondence room where sat Paul, Peter, James and John penning their Epistles.

"I stepped into the throne room of the Revelation, where towered the glittering peaks, and got a vision of the King sitting upon the throne in all His glory, and I cried:

> All hail the power of Jesus' Name,
> Let angels prostrate fall,
> Bring forth the royal diadem
> And crown Him Lord of all."

* * * *

A. *OBJECT OF THE LESSON*

    1. To show the Word of God as a necessity in our lives for it is the very foundational spoke of effective Christian living and is God's means of communicating Himself and His truths to us.

    2. To show the necessity of prayer for communication with our heavenly Father; for provision for our needs; and for showing our dependence upon and trust in God.

B. *DISCUSSION QUESTIONS*
  QUESTIONS ON THE WORD

    1. How does the Word of God build faith? (Rom. 15:4, Phillips)

    2. How could loving God's laws (Psa. 119:165) bring peace?

3. In I Peter 2:2, what is the significance of the Word being referred to as "milk"? (food for spiritual babies.)

4. Using Heb 5:11-14, explain the difference between the "meat' and' "milk" of the Word.

5. Is one's spiritual "age" determined by the number of years he/she has known Christ? (no—by his intake and application of the Word. One may have known Christ for many years and still be a spiritual babe because he/she has never fed upon the Word of God by which we grow.)

6. What is the objective of taking in the Word of God? (James 1:22—to change our lives.)

(The Word is emphasized more in detail in Chapter VI)

QUESTIONS ON PRAYER

1. Define prayer.

2. What are some reasons for praying other than the ones listed in your study?

3. What does it mean to pray "in Jesus' name"? (This is the validating signature on the bank account of heaven. It means asking in accord with Him; asking what you—to the best of your knowledge—believe to be in accordance with His will and His Word.)

4. Why do you think prayer is such hard work?

5. If we have prayed about something a few times and have not gotten an answer, should we conclude we didn't have enough faith and stop praying? (No. Matthew 7:7—Jesus says to keep on asking, keep on knocking—and to do that and *wait* is the expression of *faith*, not quitting after praying once or twice. Luke 18:1)

6. What are some reasons people don't pray? (sin, laziness, etc.)

7. Why do you think God instituted prayer as a way to meet our needs? (Because He is God and that's what He wanted to do, and so that we'd learn to depend upon Him.)

8. Is prayer the act of getting God to agree with our desires? (No, it is submitting to His will and asking Him to do His desires. I Jn. 5:14,15)

9. If prayer is asking God to do what He wants done anyway, then what is our part? (Being a cleansed, spirit-filled channel that He can use to accomplish His will. (Is. 59:1,2) All spiritual prayer originates in heaven and comes to us through the Holy Spirit.)

10. What should you do when you don't feel like praying? (Admit it to God and pray anyway.)

11. What do you feel is the greatest hindrance to your prayer life?

12. What ways have you found to use a prayer list?

13. What is the primary prerequisite for answered prayer? (Matt. 6:33)

C. SUGGESTIONS FOR CONCLUSION

1. Your lesson stated three reasons the Word of God is ineffective in a life. Do you remember these reasons? (Page 17—neglect, doubt, disobedience). If the Word is ineffective in your life, which of these reasons apply?

2. Perhaps your problem is a lack of *appetite* for the Word. Several things can cause loss of appetite. For instance:

   (1) Eating (Taking in Spiritual food), without *exercise* (giving out to others). Are you sharing the Word with others?

   (2) *Lack of "fresh air"* (prayer) also dulls the appetite.

   (3) *Substitutes* take the edge off our appetites. Are you substituting good things for time with the Lord in His Word?

(4) *Eating alone* also dulls the appetite. We need fellowship with others of like mind to whet our appetites.

(Notice how all three spokes—witnessing, prayer, fellowship—affect the Word spoke)

Quietly spend a few moments meditating on these reasons why the Word of God is ineffective in your life or why you have no real appetite or hunger for it. Then invite the ladies to talk to God about these needs as you spend time in prayer. Share the following with them:

"Thou are coming to a King
Large petitions with thee bring
For His love and power are such
None can ever ask too much."
(Author unknown)

D. *ADDITIONAL SCRIPTURES*
II Cor. 3:18; Ps. 119:9,11; Mark 11:24

E. *POSSIBLE PROJECTS*
1. Start an organized Bible reading program of your own, if not already doing it.
2. Make a prayer list and look for a verse of scripture to fit each request.
3. Choose a prayer partner and share with that one something from the Word or an answer to prayer this week.
4. Listen to Tape 262 by Jim Downing entitled, "Prayer." List his practical points to praying and apply two of them in your own prayer life this week.

F. *EXTRA HELPS*
Power through Prayer by E. M. Bounds
Master Secrets of Prayer by C. V. Thompson, Back to the Bible Publishers
Prayer or Pretense by J. A. Hanne
Sense and Nonsense by Lehman Strauss
Tape 2257—**"Prayer"**
Tape 262—**"Prayer"**

THE CHRIST-CENTERED LIFE
(WHEEL ILLUSTRATION)

PART III—The Horizontal Outreach Spokes

* Note: In Chapter V on Lordship we will be suggesting an application taken from a little booklet called "My Heart, Christ's Home" by Dr. Robert B. Munger. It would be good to have these to pass out as you begin in Chapter V. We suggest you call a Christian bookstore near you and see if they carry this booklet. If not, you may order them from:

The Billy Graham Evangelistic Association
Box 779
Minneapolis, Minnesota

In last week's lesson we studied the vertical spokes of the Wheel, having to do with our relationship with God. In this week's study we consider the horizontal spokes, which have to do with our relationship with people. For many Christians both of these areas of fellowship and witnessing are very weak or lacking altogether.

Ask God to use this Bible study and the class discussion to show each one what her individual needs are in these areas and that she would take steps *now* to correct them, in obedience to God.

Playing the tape "Link in the Chain" (Tape BSU-170) mentioned in the Godly Woman (page 23), would be an excellent way to begin, or end, this class. It is brief and very powerfully shows the effect of a faithful witness.

A. *OBJECT OF THE LESSON*

1. To help your group realize the importance of Christian fellowship and sharing their faith.

2. To motivate them to seek to strengthen fellowship and to witness effectively.

B. DISCUSSION QUESTIONS
QUESTIONS ON FELLOWSHIP

1. What do you understand the four things listed in Acts 2:42 to mean?

2. How did you answer question 5 on page 19 in your study? (Col. 2:18, 19 Living Bible; Eph. 4:16 in the 20th Century New Testament says: "For from him the whole Body, closely joined and knit together by the contact of every part with the source of its life, derives its power to grow, in proportion to the vigor of each individual part; and so is being built up in a spirit of love.")

3. What are some results of "sharing the common life"?

4. What are some special times when fellowship can be nurtured and built up and strengthened? (during a time of illness, or death, or some other time of need.)

5. Why do you feel fellowship is important? (a) for mutual support—Ecc. 4:9,10; Heb. 3:13 (b) for increased prayer effectiveness. Matt. 18:19,20 (c) for increased ministry effectiveness. Lev. 26:8; (d) for mutual edification Prov. 27:17; (e) for motivation Prov. 27:17: Ecc. 4:9,10. (f) precious to God. Mal. 3:16. (g) fulfills Jesus' prayer for unity. John 17.

6. Could someone share an experience where you were helped by Christian fellowship—or where you were hindered due to the lack of any Christian fellowship?

7. According to Col. 3:14-16 what are some ingredients of godly fellowship?

QUESTIONS ON WITNESSING

1. What are you doing now in the way of consistent personal evangelism?

2. Define the word "witness" (one who tells what he has seen, heard, or experienced.)

3. What qualifications do you consider important for an effective Christian witness? (must know Christ

personally yourself, be *willing* to share what Christ has done for you and what He wants to do for others, be *available* to Him.)

4. Read your testimony as you wrote it for question 7 on page 21. (Have the class members comment on whether each one included the three basic elements mentioned, whether it was clear, etc.)

5. Pair up and practice sharing "Steps to Peace with God."

C. *SUGGESTIONS FOR CONCLUSION*

Now that we've studied each part of the Wheel, let's think in closing, about the Wheel as a whole.

1. How important is *balance* in the Christian life as represented by the Wheel? What if the hub is not in the center of the wheel? (Wheel out of balance and useless)

2. What if one spoke is longer or shorter than the others —or one spoke is missing altogether? (The Wheel is lopsided, out of balance, cannot function properly)

3. Draw a picture of what you think the Wheel of your life looks like at this point.

4. What will you do this week to bring it into balance?

D. *ADDITIONAL SCRIPTURES*

II Tim. 2:2; Col. 1:28,29; Prov. 27:17; Prov. 12:18 (LB); Rev. 12:11; I Pet. 3:15; Rom. 1:11,12; I Cor. 9:16; Acts 20:24; Col. 4:3-6 (LB); Matt. 4:19; Prov. 11:30; I Thess. 2:4; Jn. 15:8; Eph. 3:8 (LB); Romans 1:16; Jude 23, Isaiah 8:16 (LB).

E. *POSSIBLE PROJECTS*

1. Write out your testimony and share it with someone not in your family. Keep it 3-5 minutes long.

2. Learn your testimony by memory, and if it is not suitable for sharing with another, re-work it until it is.

3. Share the "Steps to Peace with God" with someone this week.

4. Get together with another Christian woman this week for prayer.

5. Listen to tape #600, by Paul Little, on witnessing. Use his approach on one person this week.

6. This week make specific plans for encouraging and strengthing fellowship with someone you don't know well or don't see very often. Invite them to your home for a meal, have lunch together, invite them to a Bible study, plan something recreational together, etc.

F. *EXTRA HELPS*

Hudson Taylor's Life—God's Man in China by Mr. and Mrs. Howard Taylor
How to Give Away your Faith by Paul Little
The Art of Personal Witnessing by Lorne Sanny
Master Plan of Evangelism by Coleman
Soul Winning Made Easy by C. S. Lovett
Tape 234—"Witnessing"
Tape 780—"Open Nerve Evangelism"

Note: The next lesson is on the Devotional Life. The booklets and tapes listed under "Suggestions for Further Study" (page 28 of the Bible Study) are excellent. Perhaps you would like to assign various ones to read one of these booklets, or listen to a tape and report on it in class as you study The Devotional Life.

CHAPTER IV
THE DEVOTIONAL LIFE

If you were to ask Godly Christians around the world "What, in your opinion, is the least common denominator for a victorious Christian life?", I'm sure the answer would be unanimous: a daily time of fellowship with God in the Word and prayer.

Then what do you suppose Satan's attitude is towards Christians beginning or continuing faithfully in a daily time alone with God?

Let me urge you, teacher, if you have never established a daily Quiet Time that you do so *now* as you prepare this lesson. And pray earnestly that this study will result in everyone in your class becoming involved in an exciting, fulfilling, deepening, God-honoring, *consistent* Quiet Time.

Before you begin the discussion questions, ask for reports on the books and tapes you assigned last week (if you did so).

A. *OBJECT OF THE LESSON*

    1. To help each one realize the importance of a daily Quiet Time.

    2. To generate in them a desire for the Quiet Time.

    3. To get them started this week in a Quiet Time (or to encourage them in continuing a daily Quiet Time if they have already started having one).

B. *DISCUSSION QUESTIONS*

    1. Why do you feel the Quiet Time is important? Here are many possible answers, not necessarily in order of importance).

        a. To know Him. Phil 3:10 (Amp); II Peter 1:2,3; Ezra 7:10; Jn. 4:23; Mark 1:35; Deut. 17:19

        b. To be like Christ. Transformation. II Cor. 3:18; Col. 2:9,10

        c. It is a way God can deal with attitudes. I Cor. 1:9; Col. 1:10; Jn. 16:7,8; Prov. 3:5,6

d. For cleansing. As we fellowship with Christ in His Word, He exposes sin in our life. Heb. 4:12; Ps. 139:23,24

e. Desperation. (need or motive) II Pet. 1:3; Luke 10:38-42; Prov. 8:17; Luke 9:23; Col. 2:2-3,6

f. For direction, guidance. Ps. 32:8; Ps. 119:105; Ps. 119:19 (LB)

g. To nurture our relationship with Jesus Christ; to cause it to grow. I Peter 2:2; II Pet. 3:18; II Cor. 3:18; Rom. 8:29; Eph. 4:13

h. It changes lives. I Jn. 1:3 (Teacher: Share your own testimony of how your own life has been changed since you have been having a Quiet Time. Invite others to tell of the changes in their lives which have come about as a result of their daily Quiet Time.)

i. The Quiet Time reveals God's love to us and our dependence upon God. Matt. 22:29; Eph. 1:8 (LB)

j. For food. I Peter 2:2,3; Matt. 4:4

k. God desires our fellowship. John 4:23; Song of Solomon 2:14

2. What time of day do you feel is best for a Quiet Time? Why?

(Teacher: Probably most will say morning—or the beginning of their day. Some however, will feel night time is their best time. Obviously the most important thing we want to get across is the importance of *having a regular*, daily Quiet Time. Actually, it is a good practice to begin *and* end the day with the Lord. For instance, those who prefer a morning Quiet Time might then end the day with quiet meditation on what they read that morning or by reviewing verses they have memorized, etc.

Those who prefer their longer time with the Lord at night should start their day with a prayer of commitment and meditation on a verse, or few verses, of Scripture.)

Some reasons for having a Quiet Time at the beginning of the day:

a. It's like putting on your armor before going out to battle.

b. It's like getting one's "marching orders" for the day.

c. It sets the tone of the day.

d. Biblical examples: Jesus—Mark 1:35; The psalmist Ps. 5:3, 143:8.

3. How did you learn about the Quiet Time?
4. How did you start?
5. What does it mean to you?
6. Explain I Thess. 5:17.
7. How does Quiet Time help us to know God?
8. How can Quiet Time allow our hearts to be searched? Heb. 4:12; Ps. 36:9
9. How can we get guidance from our Quiet Time?
10. What problems have you personally had in being consistent? How did you solve that problem?
11. What format do you use in the Quiet Time? What materials?
12. In sharing Quiet Time with another person, how would you go about "selling" them on the value, the necessity, etc. of a Quiet Time? Where would you have them start reading?
13. Which of the hindrances to daily devotions that you listed on page 24 (question 5) do you most identify with? What do you plan to do this week to remove that handrance?

C. SUGGESTIONS FOR CONCLUSION

Perhaps you might use one or more of the following to close today's study (or to intersperse throughout the study).

TAKE TIME TO BE HOLY

Take time to be holy, speak oft with thy Lord;
Abide in Him always, and feed on His Word.
Make friends of God's children, help those who are weak,
Forgetting in nothing His blessing to seek.

Take time to be holy, the world rushes on;
Spend much time in secret with Jesus alone.
By looking to Jesus, like Him thou shalt be;
Thy friends in thy conduct His likeness shall see.

Take time to be holy, let Him by thy guide.
And run not before Him, whatever betide.
In joy or in sorrow still follow thy Lord,
And looking to Jesus still trust in His Word.

Take time to be holy, be calm in thy soul.
Each thought and each motive, beneath His control;
Thus led by His Spirit to fountains of love,
Thou soon shall be fitted for service above.

William Longstaff

MORNING WATCH

"And in the morning, rising up a great while before day, he went out and departed into a solitary place, and there prayed." Mark 1:35

I met God in the morning
When the day was at its best,
And His presence came like sunrise,
Like a glory within my breast.

All day long the Presence lingered,
All day long He stayed with me;
And we sailed in perfect calmness
O'er a very troubled sea.

Other ships were blown and battered,
Other ships were sore distressed;
But the winds that seemed to drive them
Brought to us a peace and rest.

Then I thought of other mornings,
With a keen remorse of mind,
When I too, had loosed the moorings
With His Presence left behind.

So I think I know the secret
Learned from many a troubled way;
You must seek God in the morning
If you want Him through the day.

Bishop Ralph Cushman

THE READER

She read the "Journal" and the "Post,"
  The "Green Book" and the "Red,"
She kept the serials of the month
  Securely in her head.

She went through books both old and new,
  Best-sellers, too, she thought;
She read the jokes and studied styles;
  No item went for naught.

She read the sporting page; she knew
  Each athlete by his name;
She read of baseball, football, golf—
  Familiar with each game.

She looked the funny paper through;
  She watched the mails to seize
The magazine she liked the best,
  Whose columns most did please.

But in her house there was a Book
  With pages never turned,
Whose messages of truth and hope
  Were still by her unlearned—

The Book that tells of Him who came
  To earth that we might know
The beauty of a sinless life,
  Lived here so long ago.

What pity 'tis she does not know
  This Man of Galilee,
Who healed the lame, the blind, the deaf,
  Beside the sapphire sea!

And still she reads and laughs and cries
  O'er stories of the hour;
And lets the Book, dust covered, lie
  Unopened in its power.

And still the Book, dust-covered, lies,
  Its pages never turned;

Its messages of truth and hope
   Are by her yet unlearned.

And shall we not a lesson glean
   From readers such as she?
Be this our favorite Book that tells
   Of Christ of Galilee!

Author unknown.

PRAYER

Prayer is so simple,
It is like quietly opening a door
And slipping into the very presence of God,
There in the stillness
To listen for His voice—
Perhaps to petition,
Or only to listen—
It matters not.
Just to be there
In His presence
Is prayer!

Author unknown

THINK OF OUR LORD SPEAKING TO YOU AND SAYING . . .

"You do not have to be clever to please me; all you have to do is to want to love me. Just speak to me as you would to anyone of whom you are very fond.

"Are there any people you want to pray for? Say their names to me, and ask of me as much as you like. I am generous and know all their needs, but I want you to show your love for them and me by trusting me to do what I know is best.

"Tell me about the poor, the sick, and the sinners, and if you have lost the friendship or affection of anyone, tell me about that, too.

"Is there anything you want for your soul? If you like you can write out a long list of all your needs, and come and read it to me.

"Just tell me about your pride, your touchiness, self-centeredness, meanness and laziness. Do not be ashamed; there are many saints in Heaven who had the same faults as you; they prayed to me and, little by little, their faults were corrected.

"Do not hesitate to ask me for blessings for the body and mind; for health, memory, success. I can give everything, and I always do give everything needed to make souls holier.

"What is it that you want today? Tell me, for I long to do you good. What are your plans. Tell me about them. Is there anyone you want to please? What do you want to do for them?

"And don't you want to do anything for me? Don't you want to do a little good to the souls of your friends who perhaps have forgotten me? Tell me about your failures, and I will show you the cause of them. What are your worries? Who has caused you pain? Tell me all about it, and add that you will forgive and forget, and I will bless you.

"Are you afraid of anything? Have you any tormenting, unreasonable fears? Trust yourself to me. I am here. I see everything. I will not leave you.

"Have you no joys to tell me about? Why do you not share your happiness with me? Tell me what has happened since yesterday to cheer and comfort you. Whatever it was, however big, however small, I prepared it. Show me your gratitude and thank me.

"Are you determined to run into no temptations? Have you made up your mind about bad books and bad friendships? They disturb the peace of your soul. Are you going to be kind to that one who has hurt you?

"Well, go along now. Get on with your work. Try and be quieter, humbler, more submissive, kinder; and come back soon and bring me a more devoted heart. Tomorrow I shall have more blessings for you."

D. ADDITIONAL SCRIPTURES

Is. 50:4; Lam. 3:22,23; Matt. 6:11; Matt. 21:22; Acts 20:32; Hos. 6:3; Rom. 12:1,2; Prov. 8:17; II Cor. 4:16; Gen. 5:21-24; I Thess. 2:13; I Jn. 3; Is. 59:1,2 (NEB); I Jn. 1:10; II Peter 1:4; Ps. 119:8 (LB); James 1:23,24; Heb. 4:12; Phil. 3:10; Luke 24:27; I Tim. 4:15; John 10:10.

E. POSSIBLE PROJECTS

1. Form a "partnership" with someone with whom you can share your Quiet Time blessings every day this week.

2. Share the idea and method of Quiet Time with some-one else this week.

3. Have the ladies share what God has shown them by using the "Spiritual SPECS" during each day's reading:
   S—Sins to forsake.
   P—Promise to claim
   E—Example to follow
   C—Commands to obey
   S—Stumbling blocks or errors to avoid.

4. Have them write down any new thoughts about God.

F. EXTRA HELPS

Tape 822—"Quiet Time"
The Abundant Life by Ray E. Baughman
Prayer—Conversing with God by Rosalind Rinker
The Christian Secret of a Happy Life by Hanna Smith
Think of our Lord Speaking to You by Mirfield Publications

CHAPTER V

THE LORDSHIP OF CHRIST
(Death to the Self-Life)

Teacher, let me share with you today a description of Christ as Lord, as given by S. M. Lockridge. (Tape #1206—"The Lordship of Christ"). Meditate on this prayerfully as you prepare this lesson and I believe your heart will be deeply blessed I'm sure your ladies would enjoy it also. (You may wish to play this part from the tape by Mr. Lockridge as the introduction for this lesson on Lordship).

"He is the Master of the mighty—

He is the Captain of the conquerors—

He is the Head of the heroes—

He is the Leader of the legislators—

He is the Overseer of the overcomers—

He is the Governor of the governors—

He is the Prince of princes—

He is the King of kings and Lord of lords!

He is owner!—Even though He did not
have to put His signature in the sunset—**He is
still owner!**

Even though He did not stamp a laundry mark on
the meadow—**He is still the owner!**

Even though He did not have to carve His initials
in the side of the mountain—**He is the owner!**

He did not have to put a brand on the cattle of
a thousand hills—but **He's the owner!**

He did not have to take out a copyright on the songs
He gives the birds to sing—but **He's
the owner!**

His Lordship is based on His **ownership. He is
Lord!**"

A. *OBJECT OF THE LESSON*

1. To help each one face the fact of Christ's right to be Lord of her life.

2. To respond positively by taking definite action in that direction.

B. DISCUSSION QUESTIONS

1. This subject, "The Lordship of Christ", is one which is known by many different terms in different Christian circles . . . such as: The Spirit-filled life, the exchanged life, consecration, total surrender, re-dedication, etc. I would encourage you to take time at the beginning of this class to hear the different definitions or explanations of what the women feel is meant by "The Lordship of Christ." Perhaps together you can then formulate a definition which all of you understand and agree upon.

2. Does Matthew 6:24 give any new insight into the matter of Lordship?

3. What does it mean to live to God's glory? How would you define "glorify"? (To glorify means: to enhance the reputation of. Hence, when we say we are glorifying God or living to God's glory, this means we are enhancing the reputation of God.)

4. What areas of life are included in "Lordship"? (All areas). Let's name as many of these specific areas as we can think of. (e.g. Uncommitted ambitions, loved ones, home, children, future, careers, fears, habits, my "rights", money, talents, and "bosom sins"—little things we think are hidden and unnoticed—like resentment, anger, envy, negative attitude, critical spirit, etc.).

5. What does it mean to deny self? How does this differ from self-denial? (*Self-denial* means to deny some personal pleasure or desire—e.g. denying yourself a second piece of cake. *Denying self* is turning your back on, and saying "no" to the old self nature within you and saying "yes" to Christ.

—33—

C. SUGGESTIONS FOR CONCLUSION

Remind them of the booklet you asked them to read a couple of weeks ago—"My Heart, Christ's Home". (Have your own copy handy.) Ask them to name the various rooms in this heart home. Then say: "Now as we close today's lesson, I'd like you to draw out the floor plan of *your* heart. Color your rooms (the ones you control) black, and Christ's rooms (where He is clearly in control) white."

(Give them time to do this.) Then ask: "Is Christ Lord of *every* room in your heart? Has He revealed some uncommitted area to you which you weren't aware of before? Or perhaps an area which you had once committed to His Lordship but you realize now you have taken back? Will you give Him *all* the black areas of your life right now? Let's pray."

(Or perhaps you might ask them to write out their own prayer of commitment.)

D. ADDITIONAL SCRIPTURES

Col. 1:17; Psalm 73:25; Psalm 23; Romans 13:14; Mark 8:35; II Cor. 5:14,15.

E. POSSIBLE PROJECTS

1. Listen to Stephen Olford's tape "Secret of Living" (Tape 899B). Then answer this question: "What is the difference in having Christ as Savior and having Him as Lord"?

2. Make a chart showing each area of your life. For each area, show what percentage Jesus has control of and what percentage the world has control of.

3. Ask the class members to write the answer to this question:
"Who or what has the greatest single influence on my behavior and why"?

F. *EXTRA HELPS*

Fox's Book of Martyrs
Saving Life of Christ by Major Ian Thomas
My Heart, Christ's Home by Dr. R. B. Munger
Tape 2122—"Total Surrender"
Tape 1206—"Lordship"
Tape 2250—"Submission to Sovereignty; Control of thoughts; moods; affections"

CHAPTER VI

THE IMPORTANCE OF GOD'S WORD
(THE HAND)

One of Christianity's most beloved hymns is "Trust and Obey". This hymn reminds us there is no other way to be happy in Jesus, but to trust and obey. But so often we forget the only way we learn to *trust* and *obey* is "when we walk with the Lord in the *light of His Word.*" Another song we sing is "Standing on the Promises of Christ my King"—but how many promises do you know to stand on? And are you well enough acquainted with the One who made these promises to believe them and rest on them? The only way we can know and claim His promises, and trust and obey Him, is to *know His Word!* People marveled at the maturity and understanding of a young girl who had only been a Christian for two weeks. But in that two weeks she had read the New Testament through *two* times!

Teacher, today you have the privilege of being God's instrument to impart to your class the tremendous importance and absolute necessity of learning to know the Word of God by every means possible, and of the blessings that come to a life saturated with the Word. The words of "Break Thou the Bread of Life" would make a good prayer for starting today's class.

BREAK THOU THE BREAD OF LIFE

Break Thou the bread of life, Dear Lord, to me,
As Thou didst break the loaves beside the sea;
Beyond the sacred page I seek Thee, Lord,
My spirit pants for Thee, O living Word.

Bless Thou the truth, dear Lord, to me, to me,
As Thou didst bless the bread by Galilee;
Then shall all bondage cease, all fetters fall;
And I shall find my peace, my All in all.

Thou art the bread of life, O Lord, to me,
Thy holy Word the truth that saveth me;
Give me to eat and live with Thee above;
Teach me to love Thy truth, for Thou art love.

O send Thy Spirit, Lord, now unto me,
That He may touch my eyes, and make me see:
Show me the truth concealed within Thy Word,
And in Thy Book revealed I see the Lord.

Mary Ann Lathbury

A. OBJECT OF THE LESSON

1. To motivate Christians with the *necessity* of feeding on God's Word.
2. To acquaint them with the 5 ways of learning God's Word.
3. To get them to commit themselves to take in God's Word by *all* of these five methods.

This lesson covers the five ways of taking in God's Word. In the Godly Woman study, the illustration of the HAND is given. Probably many of your class members have never seen this HAND illustration. So we suggest you begin the class by giving them a visual demonstration of how one gets a better grasp on the Word of God as each of these fingers is added.

For instance: You might take your Bible and try to hold it between your small finger (which is the *hearing finger* on the HAND illustration) and the palm of your hand. Point out when one only *hears* the Word of God, there is no way to really get a grasp on it. Then if you add *reading* to this, you have a two-finger grasp—but still it is easily pulled out of your hand. If you add *study* to this (so you have hearing, reading, studying)—you now have a three finger grasp . . . and yet the Word of God can still be taken from your hand, or from your grasp. But now add the fourth finger—*memorizing*. If you are hearing it, reading it, studying it, and memorizing it, you now have a pretty good grasp on the Word of God. (Hold it between all four fingers now and the palm of the hand.) It is very difficult to pull it away. When *meditation* (the thumb) is added to the four fingers, you have a *good grip* on the Word of God. The thumb is our "grasper"—and using it in combination with any finger increases our ability to grasp something. For instance, if you meditate on what you *hear*, your grasp of what you heard will increase. Likewise, if you read the Bible and meditate on it, study it and meditate on it, memorize it and meditate on it, then you will have the kind of a "grip" or "grasp" on the Word of God which cannot be taken away from you. You know how difficult it is to grasp anything without using our thumbs . . . and so it is in the spiritual life. Without meditating on the Word of God as we hear it, read it, study it, and memorize it, it is very difficult to grasp and retain it.

B. *DISCUSSION QUESTIONS*

1. What is the objective of taking in the Word of God? (See #1 under Discussion Questions—Chapter 4—for help with this.)

2. Why do you believe all five avenues of taking in God's Word are important for Christian Growth? (Jim Downing of the Navigators says: "We need to feed (*hear* and *read*) on the Word of God to be happy Christians. We need to *study* the Word of God to be intelligent Christians. We need to *meditate* on the Word of God to be spiritual Christians. We need to *memorize* the Word of God to be skillful Christians."

As you lead your class in a more detailed study of each finger of the HAND, we suggest that you begin with meditation, since that is so essential to the other ways of intake.

MEDITATE:

1. Define meditation? ("Spiritual digestion", to ruminate, cogitate, "Chew" it over and over, to give close thought to. It carries with it the thought of *acting* upon the truth meditated upon. To consider in the mind as something to be *done*.)

2. How do you feel meditation relates to each of the four methods of intake? (We *must* meditate regardless of how we take it in if it is to be profitable to us.

3. What do you think should be our *motive* for meditation? (To get to know the Lord better through His Word. To know what and how to obey Him, etc.).

4. What does God promise the one who meditates on His Word? (Joshua 1:8; Ps. 1:2,3)

5. What should be the object of our meditation? (Ps. 1:2-3; Joshua 1:8; Ps. 119:15, 59, 60, 97; Ps. 63:6; 77:12; 104:34; Phil. 4:8)

6. Have any of you used anything that would be of practical help to the rest of us in learning to meditate better?

Here is a quote from R. D. Foster's *Challenge*: "Your dominant thought determines your present action. You become like unto that which you think upon . . . a man is transformed by the renewing of his mind. (Romans 12:2) Beware of getting alone with your thoughts . . . get alone with God's thoughts. Meditation is thinking aloud in the Presence of the Almighty. Beware of meditating on a problem. Meditate on the Word and Person of God and there you will find the answers to your problems. Beware of the danger of generalizations in reflections . . . better known as daydreaming. Get specific. Get alone and quiet with Him . . . there to hear His voice, see His face and feel the touch of His hand upon the reins of your heart. Solitude produces a quality of life that must be standard equipment for any of the Master's men."

MEMORIZE:

1. What effect do you think memorizing Scripture would have on one's mind, or on controlling one's thoughts? (Much . . . as Dr. Ernest White says: "Our characters are built in our unconscious . . . All that enters the conscious enters the unconscious!" All that we feed into our conscious minds is stored in our unconscious minds . . . Therefore, if we keep feeding into our conscious minds the Word of God and storing it there through Scripture memory, then the thoughts that come to the surface of our conscious thinking from the unconscious or subconscious part of our brain will be affected by the Word

of God.) We all have problems with the mind. There are three ways of dealing with these bad thoughts: (1) Expression—do whatever comes to your mind. (This only multiplies and compounds the problems.) (2) Repress it—ignore it. Pretend it's not there. (This doesn't work) (3) Substitution. (This is the *only* way. Phil. 4:8).

2. What do you feel are the most helpful benefits of Scripture Memory? (There are many. Here are just a few: (1) For protection, and victory over sin and Satan . . . in our life, in our minds, in our ministry—Ps. 17:4, 37:31, 119:9-11, 133; Matt. 4:4-7,10. (2) For rapid growth and strength—I Pet. 2,3; Acts 20:32; Prov. 3:1-8, 4:20-22. (3) For witnessing—I Pet. 3:15; Prov. 22:17-19; Ps. 119:27. (4) For clear guidance—Prov. 6:20-22. (5) For answers to prayer—John 15:7.
(6) Gives us the ability to do offensive and defensive battle with the Sword of the Spirit— Eph. 6:17. (7) Makes it possible for God to speak to you through His Word, anytime, anywhere, without having a Bible. (8) It is an aid to meditation—Deut. 6:6; Josh. 1:8, Ps. 1:2,3; Col. 3:16

3. What do you feel are the greatest hindrances to scripture memory? (laziness, lack of conviction that it is essential, lack of encouragement to do it and be faithful, lack of workable plan)

STUDY:

1. What do you think makes the difference between just simply reading and studying? (studying implies using pencil and paper, writing down thoughts and organizing them, cross-referencing to find the total teaching of the Bible on what you are studying, and interpreting what it says. In reading one finds whatever lies on the surface. In studying one digs beneath the surface and finds treasures).

2. What do the following Scriptures indicate as to *how* we are to study? Acts 17:11, Ezra 7:10 . . . (With a prepared heart); Ps. 119:18, James 1:5 . . . (Prayerfully);

Ps. 119:15-16, 33 . . . (With a desire to obey what you learn).

3. According to these scriptures, *why* are we to study the Bible?
   —II Tim. 2:15? (To present ourselves as approved, un-ashamed workmen)
   —Ezra 7:10? (In order to *do* it and teach it.)
   —Acts 17:11? (with an open mind ready to search all the scriptures to find the *truth.*)

4. How do you feel being a part of a Bible Study group fits in with God's desire for us to study? (Most of us simply wouldn't do it on our own.)

READ:

1. How often does God want us to read His Word? (Daily—Deut. 17:19) Why? (To remind us to fear (reverence) God, to know and do His statutes, to look at the Lord and be changed into His likeness—II Cor. 3:18)

2. Do you have trouble with your thoughts wandering when you read? Or do you have the feeling you are not grasping it or not getting anything out of your reading of the Scripture? What suggestions can we share with one another today that might help in overcoming these problems?

   Here is a good set of questions to ask yourself after you have read the Word:

   What have I read about the Lord today?
   What have I read about myself today?
   Is there a prayer I have read that I may use for myself?
   Which verse shall I choose to think about today?
   Is there an example to follow?
   Is there a command to obey?
   Is there an error to avoid?
   Is there a promise to claim?
   Is there any new thought about God Himself?

Another idea is to use the acronym—"Spiritual SPECS"—

S—Sins to forsake
P—Promises to claim
E—Examples to follow
C—Commands to obey
S—Stumbling blocks to avoid.

HEAR:

If you have time, teacher, you might wish to use these Scriptures to show how we can *hear* more profitably. Someone has called them "Hearing Aids".

1. Hab. 2:20—hear the Word reverently
2. Ps. 62:5—expectantly
3. I Sam. 3:10—prayerfully
4. Acts 15:12—attentively
5. Neh. 8:8—understandingly
6. Acts 17:11—discerningly
7. Matt. 7:24-27—obediently

1. What steps can we take to apply the Word we *hear* spoken? (Prayerfully ask the Lord to speak to me about one point He wants me to apply from this message.) (—Incidentally teacher, you might want to remind your class of the value of listening to taped messages as they drive or do menial tasks)

2. Since we retain less from hearing than any other method of intake, how can we increase our retention when listening? (Take notes and review)

C. SUGGESTIONS FOR CONCLUSION

1. Ask the ladies to share their applications. (The answers to questions 5 & 6 on page 36). As each one shares, ask each person to write down the application of the one on her *right*. When all have shared, ask each one to pray for the person on her right regarding her application of this lesson.

D. *ADDITIONAL SCRIPTURES*

Rom. 12:2; Ps. 119:96,97; Heb. 4:12; II Cor. 10:4,5; Matt. 4:4-11; Ps. 119:105; Col. 3:23.

E. *POSSIBLE PROJECTS*

1. Keep a record of how much time you spend in a week taking in the Word by each of the five methods.

2. Do a study on meditation from the scriptures by looking up all the verses you can find using the word meditate or meditation.

F. *EXTRA HELPS*

Tape 2015 & 1129—"Importance of the Word"
Tape 754—"Application of the Word"
Tape 1167—"Scripture Saturation"
Woman to Woman by Eugenia Price (Chapter 4)
Godly Self-Control by A. T. Pierson

CHAPTER VII

BIBLICAL EXAMPLE—THE SHUNAMMITE WOMAN

Today we have the privilege of "looking through a window" and observing one of the great women of the Bible—whose name we don't even know. She is only called "The Shunammite woman" or "a woman from Shunam." I always enjoy taking a group of women through this study for several reasons: The Shunammite woman is easy for us to identify with; this story is a good picture of a Godly woman functioning in her home; it shows her heart response to people, joys, sorrows, God; she is also a good subject for one to do a character study on.

So I trust, teacher, you will pray earnestly that you will be able, through the Holy Spirit's power, to bring the women in your class to a very personal application from this intimate glimpse at this remarkable woman.

A. *OBJECT OF THE LESSON*

That the women would:
1. See the Shunammite woman as an ordinary woman committed to God, significantly used and blessed of God in her own home.

2. See how they can be used significantly and greatly blessed in their own home if they likewise are sensitive and committed to Him.

B. *DISCUSSION QUESTIONS*

1. Picture yourself as a next-door neighbor to the Shunammite woman. How would you describe her?

2. What indications do we have that she and her husband were wealthy? (verse 8 says she was "great" which means of a higher class. Some translations say she was "a prominent woman." Her husband was a landowner with servants.)

3. Often Christians are insensitive or indifferent to the needs of missionaries or Christian workers—such as their tiredness, self-denial, pinched economy, and un-

heralded heroism. What was the Shunammite woman's attitude toward Elisha? (She was very sensitive to his needs. She wanted to share the warmth and security of their home, to provide for his needs and to make life a little easier for this servant of God.)

4. Such giving and sharing is never one way. What blessings or rewards did she receive as a result of her kindness? Can anyone in the class share a blessing which you and your family received as a result of sharing with one of God's servants?

5. What do you think motivated her? (love for God; a sense of what a great privilege it was to have such a man of God in their home. She had no ulterior motive—desired nothing from Elisha.)

6. What are some wrong motives a person might have for doing good to another?

7. What do you think she meant when she said "I dwell among my own people"? (The Living Bible says "I am perfectly content". Berkeley's footnote says "My people will take care of me should I need anything.")

8. From the brief account given, would you say she or her husband was more spiritually attuned? (The woman—She perceived Elisha as a man of God, she wanted to meet his needs, she thought to go to him when her son died, while the husband thought one might only go to see him on a "holy day" etc.)

9. If a wife has more spiritual interest than her husband what advice would you give her? (be loving, submissive, and reverent, don't "flaunt" your spiritual interest, be quiet and pray, don't make God a competitor for your affections and love in your husband's eyes.)

10. What do you think the Shunammite's response in verse 16 indicates? (probably incredulity and sincere questioning in light of the circumstances—her barrenness all these years and her husband's old age.)

11. What does verse 24 tell you of this woman? (Although a prominent lady, she saddled the donkey herself and didn't need to be coddled or waited on).

12. Why do you think she went to Elisha and would not be satisfied with anyone else or tell her problem to any other? (She wanted none other than the one she knew to be a real man of God; who was in constant touch with God; the one through whom God had blessed her with the son. She believed God would give Elisha the answer to her problem.)

13. What would you say is the leading lesson taught by her life?

14. What key insight about God did you discover while studying the life of the Woman of Shunam? (number VIII on page 42 in the Godly Woman study).

C. *SUGGESTIONS FOR CONCLUSION*

1. Have them share their application. (Question X, page 42). Be especially alert to any *vague* generalizations. If one is vague or general in her application, ask the others to give suggestions as to how she might personalize it. (Sometimes a person will say "I was impressed with this verse (or quality) but I can't think of anyway to apply it." Ask the group for practical suggestions.

   Go back over the detailed explanation on page 37. The application is the most important part of the study, so week after week, make sure you keep very alert to the needs in this area.

2. Ask each lady to share the trait they saw in the Shunammite woman which they would most like to see in their own life. Ask each one to pray for this quality in her life as you have a time of prayer together.

D. *ADDITIONAL SCRIPTURES*—(Teacher, these are samples of cross references you might use)

1. Hospitable—I Peter 4:9 (Phillips), Romans 12:13
2. Contentment—I Tim. 6:6,8; Heb. 13:5; Phil. 4:11
3. Trust—Ps. 37:5; Col. 2:6

4. Capable—Prov. 31:13-18
5. Persistence—Luke 18:1-8
6. Confidence—Romans 4:20,21
7. Gratitude—I Thess. 5:18; Phil. 4:6,7
8. Doubt—Gen. 18:12-14
9. Sought help of Godly counselors—Ps. 37:30,31; Ps. 16:3

E. *POSSIBLE PROJECTS*

1. Choose one or two positive characteristics of the lady from Shunam that you desire in your own life. Using a concordance or a topical textbook (like Nave's Topical Bible) find verses on these characteristics.

   Answer:
   a. Is this characteristic important to God?
   b. Should it me more important to me?
   c. What can I do to make it a part of my life?

2. Make a project out of making your home a more hospitable place to be.

F. *EXTRA HELPS*

Women Who Made Bible History by Harold J. Ockenga
MS. Means Myself by Gladys Hunt (Chapter 7)
God Speaks to Women Today by Eugenia Price
Tape 1206—"Trusting God"
Tape 1279—"Hospitality"

CHAPTER VIII

CHARACTER & GUIDANCE SYSTEM OF A DISCIPLE
(THE BICYCLE)

How many Christians have known Christ for 15-20 years and yet they are immature, baby Christians? *Too* many! As is stated in the Godly Woman Study, (page 43) it is possible to live the first year of the Christian life 20 times instead of living 20 years of the Christian life. Probably most of those who remain babes even though they have known Christ for some time simply have not known how to grow to maturity. Perhaps they have not understood how vitally important it is to *grow* as a Christian.

This is not a *new* problem. Listen to the writer of Hebrews:
"Concerning Him we have much to say, and it is hard to explain, since you have become dull of hearing. For though by this time you ought to be teachers, you have need again for some one to teach you the elementary principles of the oracles of God, and you have come to need milk and not solid food. For every one who partakes only of milk is not accustomed to the word of righteousness, for he is a babe. But solid food is for the mature, who because of practice have their senses trained to discern good and evil. Therefore, leaving the elementary teaching about the Christ, let us press on to maturity . . . " (Heb. 5:11-6:1a)

Teacher, pray that no one in your class will be able to say afterwards, "I don't know *how* to grow and mature in my Christian life." Pray each one will be challenged to "press on to maturity." Pray they will be able to discern their own character strengths and weaknesses and will take positive action to strengthen the weaknesses.

There is a good deal of material in this lesson to try and digest all at one time. You may wish to divide it into two sessions. If so, we suggest you go through question 5 (page 46) for one lesson and begin with the paragraph following question five for the next session.

A. *OBJECT OF THE LESSON*

1. To help each one discover her own character strengths and weaknesses.

2. To encourage each one to take positive action to strengthen her own character.

B. *DISCUSSION QUESTIONS*

1. How do we "grow in grace?" (II Peter 3:18, Heb 5:14, Acts 20:32. Through the Word. It is the exercise of faith, i.e. trusting God more which produces maturity.)

2. How can we accurately measure Christian growth? (By our faith and love. II Tim. 1:5. By our attitudes, response to life, our talk, our interests, the way we spend or invest time, our mind set, use of money, etc.)

3. What would happen if a person was out of balance in:

   a. Positive attitude? (Could become eccentric, and unrealistic, not facing the facts, begin seeing things through rose-colored glasses.)

   b. Drive? (Could become hard, unbending, production oriented, hyperactive)

   c. Persistence? (Could become insensitive, hold on *too* long, be inflexible)

   d. Mature personality? (Immature responses to persons and circumstances)

4. How can we personally develop each of these characteristics?

   a. *Positive attitude?* (Memorize Phil. 4:8. Believe that God is in control, He knows what is happening, He has all power, He loves you. Remember: Whatever circumstance causes you to be negative is only temporary. "This, too, shall pass away.")

   b. *Drive?* (Decide what God wants you to do and take action. Do not pamper the flesh and do not let your emotions control you. As an act of the will take positive action. Stop wasting time. When one task is finished, start another immediately. The greatest loss of time is in getting started. Eph. 5:15,16.)

DO IT NOW

He was going to be all that a mortal should be—Tomorrow.
No one should be kinder or braver than he—Tomorrow.
A friend who was troubled and weary he knew,
Who'd be glad of a lift, and who needed it, too;
On him he would call and see what he could do—Tomorrow

Each morning he stacked up the letters he'd write—Tomorrow
And thought of the folks he would fill with delight—Tomorrow.
It was too bad, indeed, he was busy today,
And hadn't a minute to stop on his way;
More time he would have to give others, he'd say—'Tomorrow.

The greatest of workers this man would have been—Tomorrow.
The world would have known him had he ever seen—Tomorrow.
But the fact is, he died, and he faded from view,
And all that he left when living was through
Was a mountain of things he intended to do—TOMORROW.

REDEEMING THE TIME

I have only just a minute

Just 60 seconds in it,

Forced upon me—can't refuse it.

Didn't seek it—didn't choose it.

I must suffer if I lose it,

Give account if I abuse it

Just a tiny little minute,

But eternity is in it.

c. *Persistence?*

PRESS ON

Nothing in the world can take the place of persistence.

Talent will not;
  Nothing is more common than unsuccessful men with talent.
Genius will not;
  Unrewarded genius is almost a proverb.
Education will not;
  The world is full of educated derilects.
Persistence and determination alone will get the job done.

Eccl. 7:8 in the Living Bible says, "Finishing is better than starting!"

"The king of Israel answered, 'Tell him; let not the man who girds on his armor boast like the man who lays it down." (I Kings 20:11, Berkeley)

Dr. V. Raymond Edman, a well known educator and writer every year would give a message to the students of his college entitled "It's always too Soon to Quit."

d. *Mature Personality?* "until we all may arrive at the unity of faith end that understanding of that Son of God that brings *completeness of personality*, tending toward the measure of the stature of the fullness of Christ." (Eph. 4:13, Berkeley). As we know Him better we mature in our personality. This is the *only* means for maturing in our personality. Col. 3:9,10 (20th Century New Testament) says: " . . . get rid of your old self and its habits, and clothe yourselves with *that new self*, which *as it gains in knowledge, is being constantly renewed, 'in resemblance to Him Who made it.'* "

5. Which of the traits do you feel is the most important and why? (From question 4, page 45)

6. Share which two traits of character you want, and why.

7. Did you learn anything new or helpful from the study of the three main areas (psychological, physical, and spiritual) which cause people to falter in their Christian life? Share what was helpful to you.

8. Let's consider some of these psychological problems which can cause us to "fall off."

   a. What do we mean by a "wrong mind set"? (Pessimistic outlook and always looking on the negative side, undue emphasis on material things, inclination to pleasure instead of obedience, and responding on the basis of the immediate and not the ultimate. Heb. 11:26. Wrong mental intake, i:e: useless garbage (soap operas, some magazines, dirty books, daydreaming) versus scripture. Proverbs 4:23).
   How can a wrong mind set be changed? (Confess it as sin, determine to do something about it, ask the Holy Spirit to fill you, take positive action to increase the intake of the Word of God.)

   b. What are we prone to be afraid of? (The unknown, the uncertain, the future, failure, etc.) What is the source of fear? (Review II Tim. 1:7 and I John 4:18 in the Living Bible) What is the antidote for fear? (trust)

   c. What does it mean to be "production oriented?" (being more interested in "measurable results" than operating by spiritual principles.)

   d. What is worldliness? (It is not a list of do's and don't's. It is an *attitude* of heart.)

   e. Guilt—How can we be rid of guilt? (By realizing that God not only forgives, but forgets each sin we confess. Micah 7:18,19 in the Living Bible says: "Where is another God like you, who pardons the sins of the survivors among his people? You cannot stay angry with your people, for you love to be merciful. Once again you will have compassion on us. You will tread our sins beneath your feet; you

will throw them into the depths of the ocean!"
Someone has said, "God throws our sins into the
deepest sea and then posts a sign there which says,
"NO FISHING HERE!' "

f. What would cause disappointment with God?
(Feeling He has failed to answer a prayer, as you
wanted it answered. Feeling He has dealt you a
low blow because of the way He made you, the environment He allowed you to be brought up in, or
the parents He gave you . . . Things that you
cannot change.)

g. Why are we often disappointed with others?
(Usually because we expect more from them than
they can or will give, or because we've gotten our
eyes off God and on to people and expect from
them what only God can give to us or do for us.)

h. Why do we become disappointed with ourselves?
(Generally it is because we don't accept ourselves
the way we are. We don't like the way we are made
(appearance); or we aren't happy with the abilities
and skills we *do* have, but rather concentrate on the
abilities or skills we don't have—things we *can't
do*; or we're not happy with the parents we have
nor the environment we live in or have had to live
in. We blame all these things for our unhappiness
and behind it all we blame God for it! So, really,
our disappointment with ourselves and others goes
back to our disappointment with God. When we
are unhappy about our appearance or skills or
parents, etc., we set up a wall of bitterness and resentment between God and us, and between other
people and ourselves. What a terribly tight,
hemmed-in way to live!) How can one change this
situation?

1. By acknowledging our bitterness toward God
for our dissatisfaction in any of these areas.
Confess it as sin.

2. Ask God's forgiveness.

3. Thank Him for the very thing you've been bitter and resentful over.

4. Determine to work *with* God (not against Him) in developing inner qualities in our lives.

i. What is meant by playing to the wrong audience? (John 5:44; Prov 29:25; I Cor. 7:23.) It means getting your self image feedback from men instead of God. When I'm playing to the wrong audience, I look to people for approval, for a sense of self-worth (e.g. "do you love me?" "Am I worthwhile?") I may or may not get back a good response. A person's response to me may come across negatively because he or she has had a bad day, or doesn't feel well, etc. When I play to the right audience (Jesus Christ) I *always* get the same positive response. Christ always says *"YES!* You have *worth* to me. You are so worthwhile and precious to Me and so loved by Me that I gave my life for you so we could be together eternally." Never do we get back any negative feedback from Him!)

j. What did you learn about bitterness and rebellion? What does it mean in Heb. 12:15 that "thereby many shall be defiled?" (Unfortunately you cannot keep bitterness to yourself. It is like an infectious disease. It affects others. It affects what you do and how you think.) Look at I Sam. 15:22,23 to see how God views rebellion). How can one get rid of bitterness and rebellion? (Ofter bitterness and rebellion are tied in with anger toward God and lack of self-acceptance, and the same four things apply: (1) Confess as sin. State specifically what you are bitter and rebellious about. (2) Ask God's forgiveness (3) Thank Him for the very cause of your bitterness and rebellion (4) Determine to cooperate with Him in developing the inner qualities you need to overcome these negative feelings.)

Teacher, it is important to point out that the most vital way to guard against "falling off" in any one of these areas, or in "getting back on" if you have fallen off is by the "renewing of the mind", that is, building new thought patterns through the Word of God. For instance, if a woman is prone to fear, she should meditate on and memorize many verses having to do with God's protection and care, what His Word says about fear, verses on how we can trust Him, etc. (II Tim. 1:7; I John 4:18 LB; I Peter 5:7 Amplified) Or if a sense of guilt is a problem, memorize and meditate on what God does with confessed sin (verses on forgiveness and cleansing such as Micah 7:18,19 LB; I John 1:9; Is. 44:22; Is. 43:25; Ps. 103:10-12; Ps. 130:3,4, etc.) Memorizing and meditating on such positive portions of Scripture rather than on the negative emotions we feel will help us rebuild thought patterns.

9. Share your answer to #7 on page 47.

10. Have the ladies turn to question 10 on page 48 and assign each person 2-3 of the statements (numbered A-L). Ask them to spend a few minutes meditating on their assigned statements and then be ready to share why these are important and how they feel these help to maintain balance and keep one progressing in the Christian life.

(Teacher, you might want to make this comment on 10C on page 48: This is a formula for making one "panic-proof"! If you believe these four things—that God is in control, that He can do anything, that He knows what is going on, and that He is personally interested in you—then you will be "panic proof"!)

11. On question 12, page 49, what two needs did you list there and why? What was your application in these areas?

C. *SUGGESTIONS FOR CONCLUSION*

Let's bow our heads and meditate on these thoughts:

1. How long have I been a Christian? Am I maturing as I should be for the length of time I have known

Christ—or am I still on "milk" when I should be on "solid food"?

2. Am I moving on toward maturity or falling off psychologically? physically? Spiritually?

3. Is there something I need to call by its real name— SIN—and confess it, ask God's forgiveness and thank Him for it and purpose to cooperate with Him in overcoming it? Is there anything I need to settle with God now in order that I might press on to maturity? If so, let's spend these closing moments transacting this business with God.

Teacher, After you have given them a period of time in which they can verbalize these prayers and commitments to God, either silently or out loud, then you might close with this reassuring word from God's Word:

"Hosea 6:3 in the Living Bible says, 'Oh, that we might know the Lord! Let us *press on to know Him* and He will respond to us as surely as the coming of dawn or the rain of early spring.' How sure is the coming of dawn? or the rains of early spring? So much *more sure* will our God hear and answer our prayers!"

D. *ADDITIONAL SCRIPTURES*

Luke 10:27; Luke 6:27,28; Prov. 28:13; Eph. 2:2; Gal. 5:17; Joshua 1:8; Ps. 1:1-3; James 1:25; I Chron. 28:20; Joshua 1:2-4; Phil. 2:5-8; Mark 10:42-45.

E. *POSSIBLE PROJECTS*

1. Determine to go to sleep each night meditating on a verse you have memorized, to help re-program your mind in one specific area.

2. Provide each person in the class with a list of good and bad characteristics of each temperament. (taken from *Transformed Temperaments* or *Spirit Controlled Temperaments* by Tim LaHaye.) Have each one check her strengths and weaknesses and determine which major group she is in. Be ready to share it with the class the next week.

F. *EXTRA HELPS*

Is Christianity Credible? by Kenneth Taylor
The Abundant Life by Ray E. Baughman
Tape 842—"How to End Well"
Tape 113—"From Pablum to Porterhouse"
Tape 980 & 981—"Plan and Power for Maturity"
Tape 882—"Going on to Maturity"
Tape 1124—"Attitudes toward Circumstances"
Tape 1167—"Scripture Saturation"
Tape 3005—"Thanksgiving to God"
Tape 2256 & 2258—"Imparting Character"
Tape 978, 979—"Problems and Peril of Immaturity"
Tape 980, 981—"Plan & Power For Christian Maturity"

CHAPTER IX

PRIORITIES, GOALS, AND THE USE OF TIME

How often have you given mental assent to the little slogan that reads: "The hurrier I go, the behinder I get!"? How many times have we said (or at least thought) "Oh, if I only had more time!" But the problem is not time, but rather *ourselves!* We so often waste time, live disorganized lives and major on the minors —and thus we minor on the majors.

In order to use time wisely we need to back up and establish goals and priorities. e.g.

1. We need to establish an overall **goal** in life. (Where am I heading in life?) as well as personal goals, goals for our families, etc.

2. Next set our priorities according to what will best help us reach our goals.

3. Then use our time in keeping with our priorities to accomplish our goals.

> "Only one life
> 'Twill soon be past.
> Only what's done
> For Christ will last."

The subject of this lesson is an area in which we all have needs. Teacher, pray about your own personal need as well as asking God to meet specific needs in the lives of your class members.

A. *OBJECT OF THE LESSON*

1. To help each one see God's perspective on time and know how to plan and use time more efficiently.

2. To help each one become a better steward of her life by helping her set measurable and attainable goals.

B. *DISCUSSION QUESTIONS*

1. What does the word "priority" mean? (indicates that some things come "prior or before" some other things.

—not instead of. Having priorities enables you to walk purposefully through life with some guidelines for making decisions and using your time to reach your goals.)

2. What does God's Word say in I Cor. 6:19,20 is the reason we need to organize "our" time?

3. Look at Mark 4:19. What things must we avoid to keep confusion and wrong planning out of our priorities? When can we be sure our use of time is not glorifying God? (When it crowds out the Word).

4. What are some practical ways to get the most out of little moments of time? e.g. while waiting for a bus or a person, drying your hair, waiting in line, etc. (Josh. 1:8,9; Ps. 119:97-99. Learn to do two things at once. For instance, iron or shine shoes and listen to a tape. Review verses while walking or waiting, etc.)

It is very easy to waste much time with a minute or two here, five minutes there, etc. We need to stop the "leakage" of minutes.

5. Do you feel in order to do God's will in one area you will have to neglect His will in another area? (No—God's will is not conflicting. God's will done in God's way will not lack God's time.)

6. Give an example of planning ahead, and the results. Give an example of *not* planning ahead and the results.

7. Why do you feel people don't get the facts? (They don't want to change their mind; it takes time and hard work)

8. What are some of the reasons for indecisiveness? (Immaturity—Prov. 17:24 LB, fear of consequences, lack of facts, fear of others, lack of convictions, lack of faith, lack of clear-cut goals and objectives).

9. What are some results of indecisiveness? (Prov. 12:25 Anxiousness, ineffectiveness, frustration, lack of accomplishment (Wishful thinking equals zero accomplishment and produces apathy on the part of those you are responsible to lead), loss of opportunity leading to

guilt—which produces poor judgment, which causes paralysis. Indecisiveness effects every area of a person's life. James 1:8)

10. What are some cures for indecisiveness?
    a. Prov. 8:5 (LB)
    b. Ask for help from God and others.
    c. Ask questions:
       1. Does God want me to know His will?
       2. Do I know it? Then act in faith.
       3. Am I trying to find His will? If not, I am kidding myself.
    d. Not to act after having found out His will is rebellion and disobedience.
    e. Trust God more.
    f. Get right with God. Prov. 28:13 (LB)
    g. Do *something*.
    h. Meditate on the Word. Romans 12:2
    i. Pray for wisdom. James 1:5 (Perspective) Col. 1:9 (Phillips)

11. What does it mean in practical ways to live with a margin? (Be realistic, allow for the unexpected. If you are to be ready to go at 6:00 p.m., plan to be ready at 5:45 p.m. This gives you a margin for the unexpected phone call, bandaging up a child's cut finger, etc. If a meal is to be ready at 6:30 p.m. plan to have it ready at 6:15 p.m. If no interruptions come, then you have a restful 15 minutes to read, review scripture verses, sit and talk with your children, or other family members, etc.)

12. How do we separate the important from the urgent? (The *urgent* can be opening the mail, seeing a treasured t.v. program, stopping to do a task you've been putting off for a month, etc. These all can be very urgent, but may not be the most important use of your time at that moment. Deciding on what you have to do, placing these things in their order or importance, and scheduling your time will help you insulate yourself from those nagging interruptions. If *you* do not plan and control your time, someone or something

else will. One very practical thing you need to guard against in this area is long visits via the telephone.)

13. How does writing things down help our time use? (It allows us to visualize the tasks before us and put them in order of their priority.)

14. Share some practical tips you use on saving time, using time efficiently, etc.

C. SUGGESTIONS FOR CONCLUSION

1. Have them look over the list of nine things in the middle of page 53 and state which two are their greatest needs. Then ask them to write out some positive step they will take this week to put these two principles into effect in their lives.

2. Ask them to look at Luke 9:57-62 and answer the following questions:
   a. What would you say were the predetermined priorities of these three men?
   b. How did their priorities determine their answers to Jesus' call?
   c. How do your personal priorities determine your answer to your Master's request?
   d. Do you also have a "not now, Jesus, because . . . " answer? What will you do to alter this situation?

3. Perhaps you would like to use the following poem, Teacher:

ONE DAY AT A TIME

One day at a time, with its failures and fears,
With its hurts and mistakes, with its weakness and tears,
With its portion of pain and its burden of care;
One day at a time we must meet and must bear.

One day at a time to be patient and strong,
To be calm under trial and sweet under wrong,
Then its toiling shall pass and its sorrow shall cease;
It shall darken and die, and the night shall bring peace.

One day at a time—but the day is so long,
And the heart is not brave and the soul is not strong.
O Thou pitiful Christ, be Thou near all the way;
Give courage and patience and strength for the day.

Swift cometh His answer, so clear and so sweet;
"Yea, I will be with thee, thy troubles to meet;
I will not forget thee, nor fail thee, nor grieve;
I will not forsake thee; I never will leave."

Not yesterday's load we are called on to bear,
Nor the morrow's uncertain and shadowy care;
Why should we look forward or back with dismay?
Our needs, as our mercies, are but for the day.

One day at a time, and the day is His day;
He hath numbered its hours, though they haste or
    delay.
His grace is sufficient; we walk not alone;
As the day, so the strength that He giveth His own.

—Annie Johnson Flint

D. *ADDITIONAL SCRIPTURES*

Matt. 6:33; Eph. 5:15-17 (Phillips); I Tim. 4:7,8; I Thess.
4:11; II Tim. 2:2; Titus 3:14; Prov. 27:1; Eccl. 3:22;
I Chron. 29:15; Ps. 39:5; Is. 38:12 (LB)

E. *POSSIBLE PROJECTS*

1. Begin keeping a pocket diary of appointments, due
   dates, plans for your week, etc.

2. Keep a notebook with you constantly for one week
   to record the ways you waste time and how much time
   you waste. Then work to stop these "time leakages".

3. Make a simple block outline of each day this week.
   Then plan your week "schedule". Write in what is
   already on your regular schedule (e.g. daily carpool
   for children, dental appointments, preparing meals,
   preparing Bible study, etc.) Make a list of things to
   be done. Arrange them in order of priority. Now fill

in on the time squares that are left according to priority.

F. *EXTRA HELPS*

Managing Your Time by Engstrom

A Spiritual Clinic by Sanders, Moody Press

Health Shall Spring Forth, Moody Press

The Inner Chamber by Andrew Murray, Zondervan

All the Time You Need, Prentice Hall

Ministry of Intercession by Andrew Murray

Tape 591, 592, 593—"Management of Time"

Tape 1024—"Use of Time"

Tape BSU 90—"Priorities and the Use of Time"

CHAPTER X

FINDING GOD'S WILL

Most all Christians have a keen interest in knowing God's will for their lives. Many earnestly and prayerfully desire to know His will in order to do it. Others only have a *curious* interest so they can compare it with their own will.

Often my husband and I are involved in seminars and conferences where the people have a number of workshops from which they may choose the 2 or 3 they wish to attend. We have observed that whenever a workshop on, "How to Know God's Will for Your Life", is offered, it consistently has one of the highest attendances.

It is very likely someone in your class is even *now* attempting to discern God's will in some area. Teacher, pray earnestly that God will use this lesson in a very significant way to give direction and guidance to all who are seeking His will now in some matter. Pray that it will put into each one's hands the necessary tools to clearly discern His will anytime.

A. *OBJECT OF THE LESSON*

1. To provide the class with tools to help them determine God's will for their lives—in large and small decisions.

2. To help bring them to a willingness to *do* His will.

B. *DISCUSSION QUESTIONS*

1. What do you think of the statement "God's will is never in opposition to His Word"? (This gives us tremendous guidance because we are great rationalizers. If there is something we *want*, and especially if we are already *emotionally* involved, it is extremely easy to convince ourselves it must be "God's will"! However, if it is in any way in opposition to His Word, we have a clear answer.)

2. Why is it important that we *know* God's will? (We can't *do* God's will unless we know it.)

3. Why is it important that we *do* God's will? (There is no other way to please God. There is no other way to be fulfilled and happy ourselves. These are two great motivators: It pleases God, and it is best for us.)

4. Who can know God's general, revealed will in the Word? (Anyone who hears or reads the Word can know His general will for all. e.g. The 10 Commandments, for all to be saved (I Tim. 2:4), to be pure and holy, free of sexual sin, (I Thess. 4:3), to give thanks in everything (I Thess. 5:18), etc.)

5. Who can know God's *specific* will for their lives? (Only those whose purpose and desire it is to do it. He does not reveal His will that we may *consider* it, or *compare* it with our own. He reveals it only that we may *do it.* John 7:17; Ps. 119:173).

6. What are the ways God leads us and reveals His will to us? (Through His Word, circumstances, inner peace, and Godly counsel)

7. What do you think is significant about Abraham's servant's statement, "I being in the way, the Lord led me"? (He was moving instead of sitting still. A moving ship is much easier to guide than one sitting still with the motors turned off. This does not indicate moving with haste or running off in "eleven different directions". What it does mean is doing everything you know to determine God's will—e.g. taking each of the steps listed on page 57 and 58.)

8. What are some prerequisites for knowing God's will that you can think of? (page 57, 58 of Godly Woman Study)

9. Can you share a time when you prayerfully sought God's will and tell us how He led you to know what His will was?

10. Can you share an instance where you *didn't* seek God's will but chose to follow your own desires and what was the result?

11. From the following verses describe what God's will is like. Rom. 12:2; Deut. 5:29; Is. 48:17,18

12. What has God promised concerning His will? (Ps. 32:8,9; Is. 30:21)

13. Describe the kind of person you would go to for counsel on the will of God.

14. What is the value of listing advantages and disadvantages?

15. One of the things we sometime find hard to accept is that it might be His will for us to suffer. What reasons can you think of why it could be God's will that we suffer?

A. To refine us. Is. 48:10
B. For His sake. Matt. 5:11,12
C. Discipline. Prov. 5:23 (RSV) Matt. 10:22; Phil. 1:29
D. To be able to help others. II Cor. 1:3,4
E. To humble us. II Cor. 12:7
F. To remind us of our helplessness. John 15:5
G. To make us trust Him. II Cor. 1:9
H. To release us from sin's power. I Peter 4:1
I. Jesus did. Heb. 2:18
J. To teach us obedience. Heb. 5:8
K. For sin. Jer. 17:9
L. Helps us commit ourselves to God. Luke 23:46
M. Can bring peace and mercy. Gal. 6:12-14
N. For chastisement. Rev. 2:10

C. SUGGESTIONS FOR CONCLUSION

1. Ask the ladies to share some blessing from this study; perhaps a specific way God has used it to help them determine and do God's will.

2. You might encourage them to write out the principles for determining right and wrong in the form of the following questions, which they could keep as a handy guide when in doubt:

a. Does the Bible speak against it?

b. Could it hurt my body?

c. Could it hurt my mind?

d. Could it hurt or cause another to stumble?

e. Will it glorify God?

   (Teacher: To *glorify* means "To enhance the reputation of")

3. You might wish to share one of the following poems in closing.

GOD'S NO

God's "no" means "Something better"—
I can trust Him with my all.
The God who formed the universe
Attendeth when I call;
And when in love and wisdom
He withholds my heart's request
His "no" means "something better".
He will give me what is best.

God's "wait awhiles" bring blessings
That His "right away's" withhold.
When He's tried me in the fire
I shall come forth as gold.
Oh, what peace it brings in sorrow,
And what comfort fills my breast
Just to know, whate'er His answer
He will give me what is best.

Barbara C. Ryberg

HIS WAY

So often we thoughtfully and carefully plan the thing
   we are going to do.
We weigh every balance and choose out the best, our
   motives well-meaning and true.
But then something happens to alter our plan, and we
   worry—"Now what shall I do?"
Then God lays another plan down in its place and says,
   "My Way is best for you."

If only when things are not just as we'd planned, we'd
    look up through each trial and test,
We'd find God's higher ways, ways past finding out,
    we'd find "His way is best."
God help us to dash every teardrop away, remembering
    what might have been true,
And smile as we think of your wonderful words, "My
    way is best for you."

STEP BY STEP

He does not lead me year by year
Nor even day by day.
But step by step my path unfolds;
My Lord directs my way.

Tomorrow's plans I do not know,
I only know this minute;
But He will say, "This is the Way
By faith now walk ye in it."

And I am glad that it is so.
Today's enough to bear;
And when tomorrow comes, His grace
Shall far exceed its care.

What need to worry then, or fret?
The God who gave His Son
Holds all my moments in His Hand
And gives them, one by one.

                             Barbara C. Ryberg

D. *ADDITIONAL SCRIPTURES*

Acts 24:16; 22:14 (LB); Ps. 40:8, 119:105; 143:10; Eph.
6:6; John 1:13; I John 2:17; James 4:15; Mk 3:35; Matt.
6:33; I Thess. 4:3,5,18; Phil. 2:3,4; I Cor. 3:16; Prov.
3:5,6.

E. *POSSIBLE PROJECTS*

1. If you or your husband have any major decisions
coming up in the next year, begin now to pray about it.

Review often the Procedure for Discovering God's Will —to make sure you are in a position to be led of God and to discern His will. Begin keeping a list of any Scriptures or evidences of God's leading in the matter.

2. If you are right now faced with a decision or problem in which you need to know God's will, determine this week to prayerfully work through each step given in the Procedure For Discovering God's Will.

F. *EXTRA HELPS*

How to Know the Will of God for Your Life, by William Orr, Scripture Press

Tape 1238—"Knowing God's Will"

Tape 68—"The Will of God and the Word of God"

CHAPTER XI

FINANCIAL RESPONSIBILITY

This is generally a subject women might think applies more to men. However, it is imperative that women also know and practice financial responsibility. For the married woman, this is part of being a helpmeet—"a helper fit for him". Financial difficulties and disagreements rate high as a cause for marital problems. For *any* women, it is essential to know how to live within an income, how to manage money, how to give, how to save, etc. How often a wife outlives her husband and is faced with financial problems and decisions about which she knows nothing.

So teacher, seek to challenge your women with the very personal aspects of this chapter and their need to be financially responsible.

This chapter is as "spiritual" in content as any of the others in the book! (In Jesus' teachings, He talked more about money than He did about Heaven, hell and eternal life combined!)

A. *OBJECT OF THE LESSON*

To teach each one to understand and apply the Biblical principles of financial responsibility in the areas of earning, saving, spending, and giving money.

B. *DISCUSSION QUESTIONS*

1. Give some practical reasons a woman needs to know and practice financial responsibility. (To be a helper to her husband, to reduce a possible area of friction and disagreement in marriage, to be able to budget, to be able to function well financially if on her own, to be a good steward, to be free rather than a slave or in bondage to money, etc.)

2. From question #3 page 60 in your study, which pitfall do you think is the most prevalent in unbelievers? Why? In believers? Why?

3. People often think, "If I just had $50.00 or $100.00 (etc.) more a month, I'd have it made! Everything would be fine! What is wrong with this thinking?

4. Look up Phil. 4:19, Mal. 3:10, and Deut. 14:23 (LB), and Rom. 12:13. Share God's plan for money as found in these verses. (To provide our needs, to show His power to bless, to train us, to bless others.)

5. What would you say are some evidence of financial bondage? (Indebtedness, constant pressure of bills, obsessed with business, desire to get rich quick, concern for temporal things) What are some evidences of financial freedom? (No past due bills, no undue vulnerability to financial pressure, proper priorities, having a margin, concern for God's work, willingness to learn from past mistakes.)

6. What can a wife's desire for more or better material possessions do to a husband? (Put him under pressure to work harder and longer hours to provide for her and thus make their marriage and home life suffer, cause him to go in debt or *more* in debt, cause friction between them.)

7. What are some dangers or negatives of a working wife? (A higher tax bracket, children and babysitter cost, deflates the husband's ego, health problems due to pressure, cost of lunches and instant food, transportation, the danger of "your money" and "my money," increased possibility of an affair.)

8. Why should we save money? (To have a margin, to be available to God, for emergencies, to help others.)

9. What are some ways you have found effective on *how* to save? (Pay God first, self second; pay cash; payroll savings, or a similiar plan where a set amount is deducted for you weekly or monthly for savings; preserve the "wind falls" (when you finish paying for something, continue putting that same amount in savings. Don't use it to buy something else!)

10. Do you live by a budget? If so, share why you feel this is essential for good stewardship.

11. What hints can you share on planning regarding how to spend the money we have? (List needs in order of importance, discontinue any services not needed, make planning a family affair, be realistic in goals and objectives, keep records, have a personal allowance for every member of the family, buy wisely—"Use it up, Wear it out, Make it do, Or do without.")

12. What are some ways we can guard against becoming financially exposed? (don't loan money, don't co-sign a note—Prov 27:13 (LB); Prov 17:18 (LB). Stay out of debt on high-depreciating items; close charge accounts; destroy credit cards; wait for God to provide —Phil 4:19; don't presume on God's grace—Matt. 4:6,8, Psalms 19:13.) (Teacher, you can expect some violent reactions against the suggestion to close charge accounts and destroy credit cards! This really goes against the grain of today's society—when everywhere we look our eyes and ears are assaulted with, "Want it, Charge it!" However if people are honest, they will admit charge accounts and credit cards lead to financial *bondage* instead of financial freedom as they promise. It is a means of presuming on the grace of God and also robs one of the joy of waiting for God to provide. Ask if anyone in the class practices the principle of paying cash only and does not use charge accounts or credit cards—if there is, ask them to tell of the blessing this is. Ask the women to take their thoughts on it to God and His word and let *Him* show them whether or not this is a sound financial principle.)

13. Does God need our money? (No. God does not need our money. He owns it all anyway. Giving is not "helping poor old God out!" God instituted giving to raise *children*, not money!)

14. Then why does God want us to give? (God demands it—Mal. 3:10; it brings great joy to God—Phil. 4:17,18; gives joy to the one receiving it—Phil. 4:10; and joy to the giver—II Cor. 9:7-10; it is good for you and a privilege—II Cor. 8:7; it is a reflection of com-

mitment—Matt. 6:19-21; others are blessed and you are blessed—II Cor 9; you get prayed for—II Cor 9:14; God gets thanked—II Cor 9:12,13.)

C. SUGGESTIONS FOR CONCLUSION

1. I believe we are all convinced now, if we weren't before, that our finances are very important to God! Of Jesus' 38 parables in the New Testament 16 deal with possessions. One out of every 6 verses in the synoptic Gospels discusses the right handling of material goods. Jesus makes our possessions—and the way we acquire them—His business. He knew we were going to have a lot of problems here! Money does not make us or break us—it merely reveals us! Is there any area of your financial life that does not line up with God's Word? If God has put His finger on any area of your finances today, will you tell Him now what you purpose to do about it as we pray together.

2. Perhaps you would like to close with the following story or poem.

There was once a ragged boy standing at Christmas time looking in a beautiful store window. But his eyes were not on the moving, mechanical toys and other bright things that normally a boy would be looking at. Instead, he looked beyond these things to a very warm pair of boots there in the window. For this little boy was standing there with nothing on but a very thin undershirt, thin trousers, no coat; his feet were wrapped with rags and you could see blood coming through them, where his feet were cracked and bleeding from the cold. A large limousine pulled up in front of the store and a chauffeur opened the door for a very finely dressed lady. She noticed the little boy as she started inside. She took his hand and took him into the store with her and began to outfit him. First of all, she got him a warm shirt, a warm cap with flaps to pull down over his ears, some stockings, and then that beautiful pair of warm, fur-lined boots in the window. As she went about outfitting this little boy, he looked up at her with tears in his eyes and said to her, "Ma'am are you God's wife?" She smiled and said, "No, but I am one of his daughters."

◊　◊　◊

Out of this life I shall never take
Things of silver and gold I make.
All that I cherish and hoard away
After I leave, on this earth must stay.
Though I have toiled for a painting rare
To hang on the wall, I must leave it there.
Though I call it mine and boast its worth,
I must give it up when I leave this earth.
All that I gather and all that I keep,
I must leave behind when I fall asleep.
And I often wonder what I shall own
In that other life, when I pass alone,
What shall they find, and what will they see
in that soul that answers to the call of me?
Shall the Great Judge learn, when my task is through
That my spirit has gathered some riches too?
Or shall it at last be mine to find,
That all I've worked for, I have left behind?

D. *ADDITIONAL SCRIPTURES*

Prov. 3:9; Prov 22:3 (LB); Matt. 16:26; II Peter 3:10; I Chron. 29:14.

E. *POSSIBLE PROJECTS*

1. Work out, with your husband, a family budget if this has not been done. Work out a plan that will enable the family to be debt free. (If help is needed to plan a budget then call on one experienced to help you set it up). For those who are not giving, make a plan to do so. For those who are not saving, begin now to save.

2. Write out a list of the basic expenditures you have for the needs of a month; then list expenses you have that could be cut or tapered. Keep track of expendi-

tures for one month and see what the unnecessary expenses are.

Destroy all credit cards and close all charge accounts this week!!!

F. *EXTRA HELPS*

Tapes 1995, 1996, 1997—"Financial Seminars #1-6"
Richest Man In Babylon by G. S. Clason, Hawthorn pub.
Champaign Living on a Beer Budget G. P. Putman's Sons (Ignore the title!—Good book)
How to Win the Grocery Game by D .D. Omohumdro

CHAPTER XII

THE CHURCH

The first two institutions established by the Lord were the *home* and the *church*. This should give us some indication as to the importance and value God puts on both of them.

The word "church" can mean many things to different people. Here we will use it in just two ways: (1) the body of believers everywhere united in Christ (2) the local assemblies of believers.

Our discussion mainly concerns relating properly to the local church and spiritual leadership in the local church.

Pray your class members will get a new vision of the importance of the church and how they fit into it. Some of the principles of spiritual leadership presented may be quite new to some. Pray their hearts will be open and receptive to God.

A. *OBJECT OF THE LESSON*

    1. To help the group understand what the church is.

    2. To relate to it properly.

    3. To understand the principles of spiritual leadership.

B. *DISCUSSION QUESTIONS*

    1. Define the universal church. (body of believers everywhere). Define the local church. (body of believers meeting together in a local assembly to be taught, built up, edified, and sent out to reach others for Christ).

    2. What is meant by "a body of believers?" (any, and all, who by an act of their will, at a point in time, have invited Jesus Christ to come into their lives and rule there as Savior and Lord.)

    3. How do you interpret I Corinthians 1:10?

    4. How are spiritual leaders often chosen? How should they be chosen? (Psalms 75:6,7)

    5. Discuss the criteria one should use in choosing a church home.

6. Teacher, give the members of your class a quiz to see how knowledgeable they are about important issues of the church they are now attending. (For instance: What are the qualifications for membership in your church? What is their stand on baptism? According to your church what is the meaning of salvation? What are works and what place do they have in a Christian's life? What is the stand your church takes on the word of God?) Point out to them that if we are giving our life, time, money and etc. to a local group of believers we should know where they stand on these issues so we will know whether or not we agree with them.

7. Where do you think you have fallen short of the fruit of the spirit in your church relationship?

8. How far does authority go in spiritual leadership (II Cor 1:24 F.F. Bruce Expanded Paraphrase says: "We are not dictators over your faith by which you stand before God.") Eccl. 8:9 NASB

9. How would you define spiritual leadership? (Spiritual leadership divides itself naturally into three kinds: the natural leadership, the elected leadership, and the God-ordained, heart-tie leadership. Natural leadership would be the father in the home. The elected leadership would be the undershepherds of the flock called by a local congregation or chosen for them by the presbytery. The third type of spiritual leadership with the God-given heart tie is a commitment of a person to someone more mature in the faith, asking the more mature to help them grow and deepen in their knowledge of the Lord).

10. How would you recognize a spiritual leader? (The way to recognize a spiritual leader is to see if he has any followers. According to Ezek. 3:17 a spiritual leader is one who faithfully shares God's message and has your best interest at heart.)

11. How can you know if someone is caring for your soul? Ps. 142:4, Is. 41:28, Is. 59:16 (These verses indicate that it would be someone who cares for you, someone

who is a counselor to you, someone who intercedes for you, someone who is sharing her life with you, praying with and for you, showing concern for you, being honest with you, taking time for you even though it costs her something.)

12. Is it important that someone care for your soul? Why? (Everyone needs someone to look to from the standpoint of leadership. Being under spiritual leadership gives us protection, helps to hold us to our highest and best, and encourages us to attempt things for God which otherwise we might not. Having someone along side to encourage and admonish us is one of God's choicest gifts to us here on earth.)

13. What is the responsibility one has who is caring for the soul of another? (to love her, pray for her, speak the truth in love—Eph. 4:15, be grateful for the privilege, determine her needs, impart ministry skills, help mold her character, be an example in pacesetting, help her share her life with others, not give up on her.)

14. What is the responsibility that one being cared for has to the one caring? (Be grateful—Gal. 6:6 Williams; be submissive—Heb. 13:17 Phillips; be teachable—Proverbs 10:8; be available).

15. How would you go about finding someone to help you? (Pray and ask God, be on the lookout for a Godly person, ask them to help you, be prepared to pay the price, realize you are not doing God or the other person a favor by receiving help—it is a privilege.) How would you find someone to help? (Pray and ask God, get your own life deep enough that you have something to share, watch for the person that keeps hanging around you—they may be the one! I Tim. 1:18 (NEB). Why is there not more of this type of thing going on? (The cost is too high.)

C. SUGGESTIONS FOR CONCLUSION

1. Share what your application is from Galatians 5:22,23

in regard to your church relationship (bottom of page 65).

Perhaps what Dr. Donald Grey Barnhouse wrote regarding these verses will be of help to you as you seek to allow God to express Himself through you in your local church situation. Dr. Barnhouse says the fruit of the Spirit is really one fruit. It is the full fruit of *love* and he expresses it in this way:

> "Joy is love singing
> Peace is love resting
> Long-suffering is love enduring
> Gentleness is love's touch
> Goodness is love's character
> Faithfulness is love's habit
> Meekness is love's self-forgetfulness
> Self-control is love holding the reins."

2. You might want to give an opportunity to the women to pray through questions 13, 14, and 15 that you perhaps used from the discussion questions with regard to their need for a spiritual leader and their need to *be* a spiritual leader to another.

D. *ADDITIONAL SCRIPTURES*

Matt. 4:19, I Cor. 12:21, I Cor. 11:1, Eph. 4:1-3, Acts 2:42, Acts 2:46,47, Heb. 10:24-25, Heb. 13:7, Heb. 13:15 (LB)

E. *POSSIBLE PROJECTS*

1. Meditate on the responsibility that one has in caring for the soul of another. If you have this responsibility are you fulfilling it well? If you do not have this responsibility now, will you make a list of the responsibilities one has in caring for the soul of another, and begin praying over them. Asking God to build them into your life and send someone to you to whom you may be of help.

2. If you are being helped by another who is your spiritual parent, make a list of your attitudes toward

this one to see if your attitudes fit the word of God.

3. Pray this week about what ministry God wants you to have in your local church.

F. *EXTRA HELPS*

God's Man in China, by Dr. and Mrs. Howard Taylor
A New Face for the Church, by Lawrence Richards

*NOTE: In preparation for teaching Chapter XV, Part I, I would highly recommend you read a small paperback book entitled *Me? Obey Him?* by Elizabeth R. Handford. (Sword of the Lord Publishers, Murfreesboro, Tenn. 37130.) Probably you can find it in a local Christian bookstore, but if not, it can be obtained from the publishers.

CHAPTER XIII
HELPING OTHERS

Have you ever had the privilege of leading someone in accepting Jesus Christ as personal Savior? Where is that one today? What help did you give? Is that one a growing Christian today—one who is walking with Christ? Or did he/she flounder and never seem to grow to maturity?

Even if a person had a healthy spiritual birth, if there was no personal help given, no loving parental care and training, there is a strong possibility they are not walking with Christ today and maturing as a Christian. Many of us did not have that kind of help, and even though we perhaps had a strong desire to grow, it was slow-going and we "fell down" many times because we had no one to encourage and teach us how to feed ourselves, how to walk, what to eat spiritually, how to grow, etc.

Teacher, pray that class members will be motivated through this lesson to follow up on anyone for whom they should now, or in the future, be responsible. Paul expressed what should be the compelling motivation of each Christian in this way, "So naturally, we proclaim Christ! We warn everyone we meet, and we teach everyone we can, all that we know about him, so that, if possible, we may bring every man up to his full maturity in Christ. This is what I am working at all the time, with all the strength that God gives me." Col. 1:28,29 (Phillips)

A. *OBJECT OF THE LESSON*

1. To teach the group the facts of follow-up.

2. To give them a hunger and desire to do it.

3. To get them involved in doing it.

B. *DISCUSSION QUESTIONS*

1. What did you learn regarding follow-up from I Thess.? (#1 page 67)

2. What is the goal of follow-up? (Col. 1:28,29)

3. What do you think is the order of priorities in follow-up? (#4 page 68)

4. What attitudes will those who are growing in maturity possess? (Phil. 3:12-15)

5. Paul was Timothy's spiritual leader. What qualities were present in Timothy's life? (Acts 16:1-4)
What was the content of Paul's training for Timothy? (II Tim. 3:10, Acts 20:4, II Tim. 1:3, I Cor. 4:17, I Thess. 3:2)
What relationship did Paul and Timothy have? (I Tim. 1:2,18, II Tim. 2:1)

6. In the light of II Tim. 2:2 who is a faithful man?

7. What training principle do you find in Mark 3:13-15?

8. If you have been doing follow-up, which one of the priorities listed under #4 page 68 is the weakest in your own life, or is the one in which you fail most?

9. What is your own greatest hindrance to effective follow-up?

10. Did you do the assignment at the end of your lesson? If you have gotten in touch with someone, share her response.

C. SUGGESTIONS FOR CONCLUSION

1. Review Col. 1:28,29 in Phillips (given in the introduction to this lesson). Ask: Is this true of your life? If not, what step do you feel God would have you take in this regard?

2. Spend time in prayer. Ask the ladies to pray for a person they are now helping, or for one they should be helping. If they feel they have no one to help, ask them to pray that God will give them someone to follow-up.

D. ADDITIONAL SCRIPTURES

I Jn 5:11, 12; Jn 5:24; I Jn 5:13; Heb 13:5b; Is 50:4; Ps 119:9-11; Acts 20:32

E. *POSSIBLE PROJECTS*

1. Take each need listed in #4 and think through a short 3 minute exhortation or explanation you could use to encourage someone in this area. Write these down thoroughly and be prepared to share them, for example:
   a. Objectives of follow-up—I Tim. 1:5 (Phillips)
   b. Personal example—Phil. 2:5-8
   c. Prayer—Luke 18:1
   d. Godly teaching—Col. 2:8-10

2. Listen to the tape "Born to Reproduce" this week.

3. Tell about the last person you followed-up. Tell what you did, what the results were, etc.

4. Contact one person who you feel responsible for or who you have tried to help and encourage in one of the areas listed in #4.

F. *EXTRA HELPS*

BSU Tape 403—"Producing Reproducers"
Born to Reproduce, by Dawson Trotman
(Teacher, this tape and this booklet by Dawson Trotman are the very finest things we can suggest for your own preparation for teaching this lesson)

CHAPTER XIV

BASIS FOR MARRIAGE

"How firm a foundation, ye saints of the Lord,
Is laid for your faith in His *excellent* Word."

God has indeed given us a sure and firm foundation for marriage in His excellent Word. But although the blueprint is clear, it is amazing how many Christians have no concept of the basis for marriage.

It is very probable you will have someone in your class to whom these will be all new thoughts—they have not been aware of God's plan for marriage. Pray earnestly, teacher, that as they study and discuss this lesson they will "see things from God's point of view" (Col. 1:9,10 Phillips)

Some, perhaps, are in the midst of very difficult marital situations. Pray they will be encouraged to walk with God and fulfill their role in marriage. Assure them, if they are being and doing what God wants them to be and do, they can claim Rom. 8:28 and know that "God is the blessed controller of all things." (I Tim. 6:15, Phillips)

Perhaps you have some who are widowed or divorced. Encourage them to go ahead and do these next chapters on marriage and the home. God will not waste this information but allow them to use some of the principles personally and share some with others.

A. OBJECT OF THE LESSON

To teach the Biblical basis for marriage so as to help each woman fill her God-given role in the family.

B. DISCUSSION QUESTIONS

1. Why did God establish marriage? (Gen. 2:18) Does this mean God meant it more for man's benefit than woman's? Or that man benefits more than woman? (No—each receives equal benefit as they fulfill their God-given role.)

2. What are some ways a husband is incomplete without a wife?

3. What scriptural principles did you find in answer to question 4 and question 5? (page 72-73)

4. What is the meaning of the word "helpmeet"? (Teacher, check the Amplified Bible and various other translations for help in answering this)

5. Can you explain the term "two become one"?

6. What parallels do you see in the marriage relationship and our walk with God? (Teacher, this is covered very thoroughly in "The Christian Home", by Shirley Rice.)

7. As you anticipated marriage which of the reasons you listed were especially important to you? (#3, page 72) Which of these reasons do you feel were of prime importance to your mate? How can you more fully meet those needs of his?

8. In your opinion, what essentials go into a solid foundation for a marriage? (Christ is the solid foundation. Then we must build love, trust, commitment, loyalty, etc.)

9. What are things that erode the foundation of marriage? (Christ not being the center, lack of love, lack of loyalty, lack of trust, etc.)

10. Why do you think Ephesians 4:26 is an important principle for a marriage? (a couple should never go to bed angry. Don't give the devil this sort of a foothold. Keep short accounts with one another. If conflicts aren't resolved quickly, they grow all out of proportion, and this promotes a communication breakdown.)

11. If you work at keeping short accounts in your marriage, what plans do you have for carrying out this principle? (Teacher, if no one mentions it, you might suggest that praying together just before you go to sleep—preferably in each other's arms would be a good plan. It's very hard to put your arms around your mate and pray if angry.)

12. Of what importance is your daily walk with Christ in striving for a Godly marriage? (It is *essential!*) Look up Ps. 62:5. How does this apply in a marriage? (Your expectations must be from God—not your husband).

13. All of us find self-centeredness (the opposite of the principle of Phil. 2:3-4) cropping up in our marriage and our family life. How does self-centeredness manifest itself in your life?

14. Discuss answers to question 6.

15. Discuss answers to question 10. Specifically the areas in which a husband is to lead. How is the wife involved in this?

16. God made men and women with different basic strengths and needs so that we can compliment, encourage, and strengthen each other, as we fulfill our roles as a family. Name some of the husband's strengths and the need this meets in his wife. What are some womanly strengths that meet needs in our husbands?

17. Ask for answers to question 11. What if the problem is he doesn't know how? What can a wife do?

18. What do you feel are the husband's responsibilities to his wife and family? What are the wife's responsibilities?

19. What if a husband isn't fulfilling God's role for him? What can a wife do? (Pray! and keep her mouth shut! Keep on fulfiilling her God-given role!)

C. SUGGESTIONS FOR CONCLUSION

1. If you have not already had the ladies share their answers to questions 7 and 16, do so now.

2. Ask the ladies to write down all their expectations regarding their husbands. (What do they expect from him? What "rights" do they think they have?) Now have a time of silent prayer and encourage them to

give the Lord each of these expectations. Then whatever He sees fit to give them through their husbands they can receive back gratefully as privileges.

3. Ask: What one thing, or one area, would you most like to see changed in your marriage? How do you think *you* (not your husband) could help bring this about? Write down "I purpose to cooperate with God to bring this to pass in our marriage by . . . . . "

4. Share with the ladies the "Ten Commandments for Wives." (author unknown to me.)

   1. Honor your own womanhood that your days may be long in the house which your husband provides for you.

   2. Expect not your husband to give you as many luxuries as your father has given you after many years of hard labor and economics.

   3. Forget not the virtue of good humor, for verily all that a man has will he give for a woman's smile.

   4. You shall not nag.

   5. You shall coddle your husband, for truly every man loves to be fussed over.

   6. Remember that the frank approval of your husband is worth more to you than the sidelong glances of many strangers.

   7. Forget not the grace of cleanliness and good dressing.

   8. Permit no one to assure you that you are having a hard time of it: neither your mother, nor your sister, nor your maiden aunt, nor any other relatives, for the judge will not hold her guiltless who permits another to disparge her husband.

   9. Keep your home with all diligence, for out of it comes the joys of your old age.

   10. Commit your ways unto the Lord your God and your children shall rise up and call you blessed.

D. *ADDITIONAL SCRIPTURES*

Eccl. 9:9; Prov. 19:14; I Peter 3:1-5; Ps. 39:1-7 (LB); Prov. 25:24; Prov. 21:19; Amos 3:3; Titus 1:6; II Tim. 3:12; Gen. 3:16; Prov. 31:10-31

E. *POSSIBLE PROJECTS*

1. Evaluate your role as a helpmeet and list ways you could be a better helper to your husband.
2. Evaluate and discuss with your husband ways you think your relationship has a unique intimacy.
3. Tell your family members every day this week that you love them.
4. Set aside a time this week to do something that you know your husband likes to do.

F. *EXTRA HELPS*

I Married You by Walter Trobisch
Design for Christian Marriage by Dwight Small
Intimate Marriage by Howard and Charlotte Clinebell
The Marriage Affair by J. A. Peterson
1 + 1 = 1 by Kay Arvin
The Christian Home by Shirley Rice
How to Succeed in Family Living by Clyde Narramore
Are You Fun to Live With? by Lionel Whiston
Tape 1805—"Husband/Wife Relationship I"
Tape 1806—"Husband/Wife Relationship II"
Bible Studies—**Two Become One** by Elven and Joyce
            Smith
            Gracious Woman by Mrs. W. D. Stuart

***TEACHER, PLEASE NOTE: I would like to highly recommend that you obtain a copy of *Physical Unity in Marriage* by Shirley Rice for each one in your class for Chapter XV, Part IV on sex. I am mentioning it ahead of time in case you cannot obtain it locally at a Christian bookstore near you, you will have time to order it from:

    The Tabernacle Church
    7120 Granby
    Norfolk, Virginia

CHAPTER XV

THE GODLY WOMAN
BEING "A HELPER FIT FOR HIM"

PART I
(FOLLOW THE LEADER)

Whenever some women hear or read the phrase "wives submit yourselves" they immediately suspect God of favoritism towards men and of great injustice towards women! They are sure God could never have had submission in mind when He said, "I know the thoughts that I think concerning you, . . . thoughts of peace and not of hurt, to give you a future and a hope." (Jer. 29:11 Berkeley)

Many women do not understand what submission really means nor that God requires it of us in order to *bless* us and enrich our lives.

Teacher, pray that women will realize God is trustworthy and will not require *anything* of us that is not for our good and blessing. Pray their hearts will be open to understand submission from God's point of view and to practice it in love.

A. *OBJECT OF THE LESSON*

1. To understand the role of the husband and wife.
2. To understand the importance of submission and the "cement" of love.
3. To be motivated to fulfill their role as a wife, in submission and love.

B. *DISCUSSION QUESTIONS*

1. What new or perhaps forgotten thought did you learn about the role of the husband? The role of the wife?
2. What did you decide the phrase "being a helper fit for him" means? (Proper, right kind of helper, completing him)
3. How would you answer someone who says, "it just won't work, because my husband does not in any way fulfill his role." (This does not alter your need to

fulfill your role. You cannot change another but you can change yourself. It is a matter of obedience or disobedience)

4. Eph. 5:24 says a wife is to submit to her husband in *everything*—What if he asks her to lie, cheat, commit immorality, etc? Are there limits to submission? If so, how do we determine these limits? (These are generally hypothetical questions—"What if?" It is important to ask two questions (1) "As a part of your wholehearted, loving submission to God, have you been living in daily submission to your husband?" (If not, then a wife is not operating by God's chain of command and is out from under God's umbrella of protection which He has provided through her husband. She cannot blame God for wrong done to her or expect Him to take responsibility for her in this situation) (2) "Has your husband ever actually required or *commanded* you to do something wrong"? I have never heard of a case where a woman is daily submitting to her husband out of love and reverence to God where the husband actually commanded her to do something morally wrong. If there was such an actual case involving a clear moral issue, then God is the wife's higher authority. The wife needs to understand God is for her, He loves her, and is trustworthy. His commands are not conflicting. God never gives two commands impossible to obey. If a woman wholeheartedly follows the Scriptures God will never make her have to choose between two wrongs.)

5. What are some ways you think a wife can be a "competer" instead of "completer?" (Spiritual activities, job, taking charge of finances, sarcasm, making decisions, dominating the conversation)

6. What does Eph. 5:22 say should be a wife's attitude in submission? (Do it as *unto the Lord*. It really has more to do with our vertical relationship to the Lord than our horizontal relationship to our husband. Remember God calls us to submit to the *position* not the personality of our husbands.)

7. I Peter 3:1 in J. B. Phillips translation says a wife is to "fit in with her husband's plans." What does this involve for you personally?

8. Let's read Proverbs 31:11,12 in several translations. What does it mean to you to be "trustworthy?" What does it mean to "richly satisfy his needs?" (The Amplified Bible says, "He will have no lack of honest gain, or need for dishonest spoil." If his needs for love, affection, companionship, sex, conversation, admiration, etc. are being adequately met at home, he will not seek these through "dishonest spoil.")

9. What definition of submission did you find that you liked best?

10. How did you answer #6 page 79?

11. Why is it sometimes hard for a wife to be submissive? (Self-will, "I'm right," it looks like being submissive would lead to disaster, he's not capable of leading, etc.)

12. Can a wife be submissive and still have a rebellious heart. (Yes—as far as the outward "act" of submission —but not as far as true submission, which is an *attitude* of the heart. When submission is an *act* it requires much discipline and self-control. It is very hard to do. But not so when it is an *attitude* of the heart.)

13. Does submission mean a wife never thinks for herself, never has an opinion, never makes a decision? (No, a wife should tell her husband how she feels, what she thinks about an issue and then commit the situation and the outcome to God, trust God and obey her husband. Submission does not mean that you always agree but you always yield. There are many decisions a husband wants his wife to make. These she should make as part of being submissive—*unless* it would clearly be against God's pattern for the role of the husband and the role of the wife.)

14. Would the way in which one wife supports her husband differ from the way another wife would support her husband? Explain.

15. How would you say two people "fall in love," or grow to love one another? (Usually the first step in a man and woman becoming interested in one another is: (1) *Awareness*—out of which comes (2) *Respect*—from which grows (3) *Admiration*—from which comes (4) *Love*.) Then how do two people fall "out of love"—or how does love grow cold and die between two people? (The cycle simply reverts unless something is done to maintain it. Love reverts to less admiration, less respect, etc.)

16. What is the source of the love described in I Cor. 13?

17. Share your definition of love. (page 82) (Teacher, you perhaps will want to share the definition given by Donald Grey Barnhouse as the end of Chapter 12 page 79).

C. *SUGGESTIONS FOR CONCLUSION*

1. Take 5-10 minutes to allow each one to think through the following questions, jot their thoughts down and pray over them.

    In what ways am I making it easier for my husband to be the leader?

    In what ways am I making it difficult for him to be the leader?

2. Have each one write out a "Prayer of Commitment" regarding submission to her husband.

3. Use John 7:17 and John 13:17 as thought conditioners before prayer.

D. *ADDITIONAL SCRIPTURES*

Proverbs 21:1; I John 3:18 (LB); I Peter 4:8; Proverbs 11:2 (Amp.); Ephesians 4:32

E. *POSSIBLE PROJECTS*

1. Take 2 pieces of paper and write the following at the top: Page 1—front—"My needs as *I* see them." Back

—"My needs as *he* sees them." Page 2—front—"His needs as *I* see them." Back—His needs as *he* sees them." Fill out the front side and ask him to fill out the back without looking at your side. Then compare. It is amazing how little we realize what our mate considers a real need!

2. Jot down requests of your husband you feel you can't or you don't obey. Is there a trend? Perhaps there is an area in which you are not willing to allow him to lead? (Example: children, finances, etc.)

F. *EXTRA HELPS*

Me? Obey Him? by Elizabeth R. Handford
The Greatest Thing in the World by Henry Drummond
Learning to be a Woman by Kenneth G. Smith
Essays on Love by Walter Trobisch
Tape 1020—"Woman's Place in Marriage"
Tape 1810—"God's Order for Wives"
Tape 245—"The Godly Woman"

CHAPTER XV

THE GODLY WOMAN BEING "A HELPER FIT FOR HIM"

PART II

(HIS HOME IS HIS CASTLE)

A castle: a place a wife has "furnished" with a good atmosphere; "warmed" by lovingly met needs and adequate, timely communication; and "lighted" by Godly Homemaking.

This castle might look like a palatial mansion or a humble cottage, or be just one room—what determines whether or not it is a "castle" is the wife that lives there!

Teacher, each section of this lesson is *so vital!* Pray that even though your timing is limited God will enable you to *accomplish the objective* and that the result will be *changed* homes and marriages—to the Glory of God!

A. *OBJECT OF THE LESSON*

That wives would:

1. Learn to make home "his castle" by the atmosphere they set—by meeting his needs, by adequate communication, and by godly homemaking.

2. Be willing to make whatever changes are necessary to reach this goal.

B. *DISCUSSION QUESTIONS*

1. What conclusions did you come to regarding the atmosphere you set in the home in the way you send him off, welcome him home, by your attitude, appearance, etc?

2. What do you think the overall atmosphere of your home is? What can you do to change and/or improve it?

3. What would you say are some basic characteristics a wife needs most to meet her husband's needs? (Self-

lessness, thoughtfulness, servant heart, etc.) Which of these do you feel is the key, or is basic to the others? (Unselfishness. Selflessness *frees* you to think creatively about the other person, to serve, be thoughtful, etc.

4. After you wrote out your husband's good characteristics what was your reaction or response to the list? Were you surprised it was so long? Did you realize you need to be more aware of his good points?

(Teacher, remind the ladies that the *negative* characteristics they see in their husbands reveal a capacity for the opposite *positive* trait. For instance, if his negative trait is being outspoken, harsh or blunt, this shows a capacity for the positive trait of honesty. Or if he has the negative trait of being too permissive, being nonchalant, this shows the capacity for the positive trait of patience. If he is stubborn, hard-headed, this shows the capacity for the positive trait of being resolute. Therefore, we can pray for the positive manifestations of these traits).

5. Did you have any experience this week of proving Luke 6:38 true in your own experience with your husband? Would you share it with us?

6. Many of us have trouble meeting our husband's need for admiration. Let's share our answers to #6 and 7 on page 85 in order to glean ideas from one another which we might use. (Teacher, here are some suggestions in case the women do not share much: *Mentally:* things having to do with his achievements, skills, and abilities—his faithfulness to provide for his family, his decisiveness in making decisions, his sound judgment. *Physically:* anything that distinguishes him as part of the male sex—strength and endurance, lifting heavy objects, managing difficult equipment, changing a tire. *Spiritually:* inner qualities God has developed—commitment, consistency, integrity, desire to obey God.)

7. How would you rate or evaluate the importance of communication in a marriage? (Teacher, be sure the ladies bring out how totally essential this is to a good marriage. If there is a breakdown in this area, it will

significantly influence and contribute to a breakdown or collapse in other areas. It is the "breath of life" to a marriage).

8. How many of you pray regularly regarding good communication with your husband? (Should be praying *regularly* to have it if you don't; to keep it and be growing in it if you do.)

9. What counsel would you give a woman who says her husband won't talk to her any more?

10. Wives generally seem to need to communicate verbally more frequently and more in detail than some husbands do, although both have a need for communication. Why do you think this is often more important to a wife? Why do you think it is important for a husband to communicate verbally?

11. How did you answer #3 on page 86?

12. Eph. 4:15 gives perhaps the three most important words to remember for good communication. What are they? (Speak, truth, love)

13. Relate some purposes of communication? (Information, decision-making, developing interpersonal relationships, for development of persons)

14. What problems or barriers to communication did you find in the Bible? (#8 page 88.) Teacher, my thoughts on these were as follows: (1) selfishness (2) pride (3) bitterness (4) anger (5) lack of concern (6) lack of knowledge (7) fear of rejection (8) shame (9) going our own way (10) heart condition

15. Share your answer to #9 on page 89. Share your answer to #10.

16. What was your response or reaction to the quote by Gladys Hunt on page 89 regarding godly homemaking? (Teacher, if they miss the point, draw from them the idea that it cannot be our *casual* interest, but must be our *major* concern—in which we must rely totally on Him!

17. Did you follow through on #3 page 90? Would you share what your husband told you, if not too personal?

C. *SUGGESTIONS FOR CONCLUSION*

1. Edgar Guest wrote: "It takes a heap a' livin' to make a house a home." J. W. Goethe wrote: "He is happiest, be he king or peasant, who finds peace in his home." Another wrote: "It takes a hundred men to make an encampment, but one woman can make a home."

   The question for us to answer today is: Have I made our home "his castle?" A place of warmth? love? peace? acceptance? joy?

   What step can I take, starting now, to make it so?

2. (Teacher, the basic idea for this suggestion comes from Shirley Rice's book, *The Christian Home*. You may wish to refer to it for more help with this and for many other wonderful ideas.)

   a. Make a list of words that characterize your concept of a home a man would consider "a castle" (e.g. warmth, unity, peace, love, cheerfulness, etc.)

   b. Then make a list of negative things that would keep it from being his castle. (e.g. coldness, bickering, discord, nagging, etc.)

   c. Now from both lists underline the words that best describe your home now. What kind of picture did you get?

   d. Go back through the list and circle the words you would like God to make true about your home.

   As we close in prayer—you bring to the Lord the things that need to be taken out of your home. Then bring Him the good qualities you need in your home to make it a cherished castle for your husband. Make yourself available to Him to accomplish these desires.

3. Helen Hunt Jackson wrote the following description of her ideal of a wife, mother, homemaker. Listen as I read it to you.

A HOME CREATOR

"The most perfect home I ever saw was in a little house, into the sweet incense of whose fires went no costly things. A thousand dollars served for a year's living of father, mother, and three children. *But the mother was a creator of a home;* her relation with her children was the most beautiful I have ever seen; even a dull and commonplace man was lifted up and enabled to do good work for souls by the *atmosphere which this woman created;* every inmate of her house involuntarily looked into her face for the keynote of the day, and it always rang clear. She has always been and always will be, my ideal of a wife, mother, homemaker."

How do you measure up? Will you pray now and ask God to make you the ideal wife and homemaker your husband needs.

D. *ADDITIONAL SCRIPTURES*

Prov. 14:30; Phil. 2:14 (Living); Col. 3:8-10; Prov. 13:10; Prov. 17:14; I Cor. 3:3 (Living); James 1:2-4; Heb. 13:5; Phil. 4:11-12

E. *POSSIBLE PROJECT*

Take one of the four sections of this chapter as your special improvement project for each week of the next month e.g.
First week—work on improving the atmosphere of the home, particularly your attitude and appearance.
Second week—concentrate on meeting your husband's needs, especially his needs for admiration and acceptance and being "ministered to."
Third week—Read one of the suggested books in Extra Helps on communication and really concentrate on improving in this area.
Fourth week—meditate on the quote by Gladys Hunt and then write down some areas of homemaking to

which you have been giving only your casual interest. Write what you will do to make this an area of *major concern*—and then do it!

F. *EXTRA HELPS*

Art of Homemaking by Hoole
The Miracle of Dialogue by Reuel L. Howe
Why Am I Afraid to Tell You Who I Am? by John Powell
To Understand Each Other by Paul Tournier
The Art of Understanding Your Mate by Cecil Osborne
Tell Me Again, I'm Listening by R. B. Wilke, Abingdon Press
Letters to Karen by Charlie Shedd
Hidden Art by Edith Shaeffer, Tyndale House

CHAPTER XV

THE GODLY WOMAN BEING "A HELPER FIT FOR HIM"

PART III

(BEING HIS QUEEN)

Last week we talked about "his castle"—this week our question is: Is there a "queen" to live in his castle? One "judged to be foremost among others in certain attributes or accomplishments."

There are many kinds of queens—beauty queens, ruling monarchs, queens in name only—but the queen we're looking for today is one who by her attitude, appearance, and character makes the man in his castle exclaim, "There are many fine women (queens!) in the world but you are the best of them all!"

Teacher, this lesson covers some areas in which it is so easy to have "blind spots" (e.g. to be blind to the fact one nags, or is bitter, or complains, or is blind to her emotional immaturity, etc.) The words to the following song expresses a worthwhile prayer for today—for you and for each one in your class.

Open My Eyes That I May See

Open my eyes that I may see Glimpses of truth Thou hast for me;

Place in my hands the wonderful key That shall unclasp, and set me free

Silently now I wait for Thee. Ready, my God, Thy will to see;

Open my eyes, illumine me, Spirit divine!"

A. *OBJECT OF THE LESSON*

1. To help the women, honestly face areas of need in their attitudes, appearance, and character

2. To desire to change in these areas

3. To purpose to cooperate with God to bring each of these areas under His control.

B. *DISCUSSION QUESTIONS*

1. Which negative attitude is most prevalent in your life?

2. Let's see if we can give an illustration of each of the bad attitudes on page 91. (Teacher, I think it would be well to discuss this list, and see if they can give an illustration of each of them to be sure they clearly understand what each one means and make sure they've matched the Scriptures correctly. The right letter for each scripture is as follows: (a) Proverbs 21:9 (b) Jude 16 (c) Proverbs 12:25 (d) Numbers 13:27-33 (e) Proverbs 18:2 (f) Hebrews 12:15

   The negative attitude they might need help in understanding is being a "dreambuster." You might use this example to help them understand it: "Your husband comes in all excited about a new idea or project and you say, 'Where do you think we'll ever get the money for that?', or 'That will never work!' or 'I read about that in a magazine a long time ago!' or 'Sue's husband made (or did) that a long time ago!'— or you show no excitement or interest in the thing he's very excited about—This is being a dreambuster!"

3. Look at #3 page 92. Explain why you think each antidote you chose is a good one for that specific bad attitude. Name some other positive attitudes you think are essential for a successful marriage.

4. What are you going to do to allow God to change a bad habit pattern this week? (#4 page 96)

5. What should be the Christian wife's perspective regarding her appearance? (How can I look my very best for God and my husband? What would please God? What would please my husband?) How could a woman tell if she had the area of personal appearance out of balance? (If she spends too much time or too little time on it, if it consumes too much or too little of her thought time.) What are some ways to keep it in balance?

6. What one part of your appearance do you feel you need to work on most?

7. Did God bring any convicting thoughts to your mind as you did the yes/no quiz on page 92? What did He say to you?

8. How do you define integrity? What does integrity have to do with our relation to our husbands?

9. In what areas do you most need to improve in the matter of consistency and faithfulness? How does consistency and faithfulness apply in our marriage?

(Teacher, to help with the section on emotional maturity I have included an article which is now out of print by Dr. Bob Munger. It is entitled "The mastery of moods" and you will find it at the end of this chapter. Psalms 42 in the Living Bible would be good to meditate on also.)

10. How did you define emotional stability and maturity?

11. Describe someone you think is stable and mature emotionally. (Galatians 5:22,23)

12. What negative emotions do you find most difficult to handle? What do you think is the key to handling them properly?

13. When you ladies are depressed, or down in the dumps, what do you find is the best remedy or solution? (Sometimes just good physical exercise will do wonders, sometimes one needs a good time alone with the Lord, sometimes doing something for someone else— getting your mind off yourself, sometimes getting a good rest, etc. Knowing the cause of the depression (whether it is physical, spiritual, mental, or emotional) helps in determining the remedy. For instance, if you are exhausted from a long period of uninterrupted labor, a good night's sleep—or getting away for a rest, will do wonders to lift the spirits. If one is depressed from self pity, feeling sorry for oneself, etc., then the best way to lift the spirits is to do something for someone else. Do something to minister to the needs of another instead of self!).

14. Look at Romans 8:28-39. What do you find here

that would help you overcome depression? (Teacher, you might want to suggest the following application of Romans 8:28 to help them anytime they are discouraged, depressed, down in the dumps—or just need to have their spirits lifted and get their eyes off "poor me!"):

a. Take a blank sheet of paper and write out the paraphrase of Romans 8:28 as it is given in the Living Bible: "And we know that all that happens to us is working for our good if we love God, and if we are fitting into His plans." Romans 8:28

b. Now re-write the phrase—"And we know that all that happens to us"—Then list all your problems, setbacks, defeats, etc.—then finish writing the rest of the verse.

c. Now write the phrase again—"And we know that all that happens to us"—This time list all of your victories, accomplishments and progress, etc.—and then complete the verse.

d. Spend time meditating on this and thanking God for what He's shown you.

15. When does depression or "feeling low" most often hit you? (It is good to be alert to possible times depression is likely to hit us: For instance before a great victory, during long periods of hard, uninterrupted labor, or in the hour of success, or the hour of victory. (Example: I Kings 18:36-46 tells of tremendous victories. Then in I Kings 19:1-8 we see Elijah in a state of depression—physically overwrought; he thought he just couldn't take any more). Why does it come after an hour of success? (Pride and letting down after driving so hard, relaxing).

16. What is worry? How does it differ from concern? (Teacher, compare the definitions for these two words in the dictionary. Below are some statistics about worry that might be of interest to the class:

Psychiatrist say 70% of what we worry about never happens. 22% is not nearly as bad as we thought it would be when it gets to us. Only 8% are valid worries. So . . . our worrying is 92% inefficient!)

17. What are we prone to be afraid of? (The unknown, the uncertain, the future, failure, etc.). What is the source of fear? (Review and emphasize II Timothy 1:7)

C. *SUGGESTIONS FOR CONCLUSION*

1. Since you have been walking with Christ, in which area do you think He has made the biggest changes? e.g. In your attitude? (Changing them from negative to positive); Your appearance? Your character? (In integrity? consistency? faithfulness? emotional stability and maturity?)

2. In which area do you see your greatest need for improvement? (Ask class to write these down as each shares. Then ask each one to pray for this area of need for each of the others in class.)

D. *ADDITIONAL SCRIPTURES*

I Peter 2:3-5; Eph. 2:10; II Cor. 10:12; Prov. 14:30 (Amp.); John 16:33; Ps. 42.

E. *POSSIBLE PROJECTS*

1. List the negative attitudes you have a problem with. One by one look these up in a concordance or Topical Textbook to see what God says about it, what He tells you to do about it, how He can change it.

2. Ask your husband how he likes you to dress casually, for dress-up, for bed, etc. Then seek to diligently follow his desires.

3. Since we become like those we are around, ask God to show you someone strong in a positive attitude or trait of character you are weak in then seek to be around that one.

F. *EXTRA HELPS*

Romances and Intrigues of the Women of the Bible by
James Faulkner

God Speaks to Women Today by Eugenia Price

**The Women of the Bible: The Life and Times of All The
Women of the Bible** by Herbert Lockyer, Zondervan

Tape BSU 65—"Honesty"

Tape 1124—"Attitudes toward Circumstances"

Tape 118—"Discouragement and Depression"

Tape 933—"God's Answer for Discouragement; for Disappointment"

Tape 310—"Emotional Conflicts vs. Physical Health"

THE MASTERY OF MOODS

by Dr. Robert Boyd Munger

" . . . to give them beauty for ashes, the oil of joy for mourning, the garment of praise for the spirit of heaviness . . ."
—ISAIAH 61:3

We are all subject to moods, some people more than others. Temperaments vary and dispositions differ, but all of us know recurring periods of depression. One may be by disposition melancholic and easily plunged into pessimism. Another may be irritable, jumpy, a constant worrier. Yet another person may be easy-going and naturally optimistic. I remember a friend once saying to me, "I never get discouraged. I am always optimistic about everything." I said to myself, "You are the exception to the rule." Most of us have our moments of discouragement and I confess that there have been times in my experience when I have known dark purple depression.

I remember particularly the teen-age years of exquisite suffering! Not long ago I came across an old diary which I had begun to keep in my sophomore year at the University—a really difficult year under any circumstances. The diary had been given to me as a Christmas gift and I kept if for about four weeks, which is longer than I have ever kept any diary. As I perused the pages I was impressed by the complete pessimism and skepticism that was mine in those days. I was critical of everything and everybody and, most of all, myself. I had no reason to be depressed. I had everything a young man could want and yet I knew depression. Thank God the "dark night of the soul" did not last and I am grateful that there came the "light of the glory of God in the face of Jesus Christ."

I have learned through the years, however, that moods will return. They may not have the same intensity or duration. They may not have the same cause but they will come, and if we do not know how to handle them or how to rely upon the grace of God, they can easily rob us of peace and joy.

Perhaps you too have a battle with your moods. Old Giant Despair comes around and throws you into Doubter's Castle. Discouragement takes you by the scruff of the neck and shakes you until your bones rattle. Fear lays its icy hand upon you until you cower in a corner. A feeling of failure and guilt puts you in some dark cell without a ray of light. Well, let us consider some sound steps in the mastery of our moods.

First, do not take your feelings too seriously. Feelings are not fundamental in life. Life is to be grounded upon fact—the sound, solid unchangeable fact of God in Christ. Life is to be anchored and oriented there. Moods and emotions come and go. The art of living is to proceed calmly, faithfully, purposefully in the light of God, no matter how you feel. Sometimes our feelings move along with us and are an encouragement, and sometimes they drag their feet and are a real discouragement. But whatever our feelings or moods, they are not fundamental. The fundamentals are the facts, and the primary facts are the way God feels about you and what He has done for you.

A student, whose term paper was due, wrote a note to his professor which read, "Dear Sir, I just did not feel up to that kind of creative effort this week." The professor called him to his office and said, "Young man, don't you know that most of the real work in this world is done by people who don't feel like doing it?" Don't take your feelings too seriously. They are incidental, not fundamental.

Don't take yourself too seriously. There are far greater issues in this old world than your happiness and your peace of mind. I think this needs to be said today because there is so much being printed on the subject of happiness and peace of mind. We get the idea that these are the big things in life. They are important but they are not of prime importance. What is the primary purpose of your being here? Why have you been brought into existence? Why did God give Himself in Jesus Christ for your redemption at such infinite cost, and if you are a believer, why has God given you new life in Him? God has done this to bring you to Himself forever. When you understand this fact you begin to place your little ideas in the light of God's eternity. You begin to understand what lies behind your existence and what lies behind the grace of God which has come to you in Christ. Life starts to balance up.

Let's start with the facts. Let us attach our faith and confidence to the unchangeable fact of God in Christ our Lord and what He has done for us, and we will find that feeling will tag along. Let's not reverse the order and think that the important thing is feeling, then faith and fact. Our feelings do **not** count. As a matter of fact the strength of our faith doesn't count. What really counts is our dependence upon God's faithfulness to us in Christ our Lord. Then come with your variable moods to God. Tell Him exactly how you feel. Say, "I am depressed. I am discouraged. I have no joy. I have no love. But Lord, you want me even if I do not want myself. You place value upon me even if I don't place value upon myself. In the Name of Jesus Christ, I put myself in your hands and wait on Thee. Give me 'the garment of praise for the spirit of heaviness'."

Moods arise from different sources. Circumstances, for example, may discourage and disturb us. An advancement is denied you in your place of business. You lose your job or have financial reverses and know discouragement. A friend misrepresents the truth or says something about you and you feel it keenly. Sickness lays you aside. A certain young lady in whom you are interested says "No," and you are depressed. A devastating blow may suddenly strike you. All right, that happens to all of us. The Gospels record that even Jesus Christ knew discouragement, for on His way into the Garden of Gethsemane when the specter of the cross was before Him, He said, "my soul is exceeding sorrowful even unto death." He felt it. His perfect humanity is manifested not in His insensibility to discouragement, trouble or suffering, but in the rapidity with which He came back into poise and power and into fellowship with the Father. When He rose from His knees in the Garden of Gethsemane He was on top of circumstances and from that moment on He was undisturbed.

He said to Pilate, "Thou couldest have no power at all against me except it were given Thee from above" (John 19:11). His last words breathed on the cross were, "Father, into thy hands I commend my spirit." He made clear to us, "In the world ye shall have tribulation; but be of good cheer; I have overcome the world" (John 16:33). By the grace of Jesus Christ, the Christian can take anything that life throws at him and make that circumstance become a stepping stone. Jesus Christ took a cross and made it a throne. He took a crown of thorns and made it a diadem. He took the reed and made it a scepter of risen power.

He took death and opened it to eternal life. This same Saviour works with us today and will do the same things for those who trust Him. Get your eyes off circumstances and on to the Saviour. Do not shrink from troubles as adversities but welcome them as opportunities.

Some moods are caused by physical illness. A continued outlay of effort and energy may result in a depletion of strength which subjects us to moods and depressions. Psychologists can chart these recurring depressions and even predict—when they know the nature of the cycle in the patient's personality and the pressure upon him—when they will occur.

The story is told of an ancient king who periodically was subject to black moods and depressions. He called his counsellors together and said, "Devise for me some simple motto which I can hang on the wall of my bedroom so that whenever I feel discouraged, I can get a lift of heart from the word." The wise men pondered this for a while and finally they came up with a motto of four words which the king hung on his bedroom wall and which always gave him a lift. The words were "This Too Shall Pass." Many of our moods are the low point of a physical cycle and they will pass of themselves. If you are in the shadows today, go shopping for a sunsuit; you will be in the sunshine before long. The Psalmist said, "Why art thou cast down O my soul and why art thou disquieted within me? Hope thou in God; for I shall yet praise Him for the help of His countenance." That is sound Christian optimism.

Some moods are caused by mental or psychological factors. These moods are difficult to handle. The sciences of psychology and psychiatry have made magnificent contributions to the understanding of ourselves and our emotions. I believe in using these sciences just as I believe in using the science of medicine. These means have been used of God again and again to bring help. I realize that for some strange reason, there are many who fear these modern sciences and feel that it is wrong to take advantage of expert counsel in these fields. It does not mean that you are a failure as a Christian or that you are mentally ill when you seek expert counsel for your emotional confusion. If one were to break a leg, he would call for a doctor to set the broken limb. There are emotional injuries which are just as real and painful as a broken limb and these need to be "set" with a skilled hand. Jesus Christ is the Master Psychologist. Let us turn first to Him. His grace and truth provide the soundest therapy for the mind and the heart. Let us place our case wholly in His hand, and then let us use the professional means He puts at our disposal that we might know the restoration which He offers us.

Some moods are moral and spiritual in their origin. The most destructive and disruptive factors in personality are sin and guilt. Ask any counsellor about this. As a minister of the Gospel it is my privilege to counsel with many people about their problems and I have seen lives literally torn to pieces by a sense of guilt. "O, the wicked are like the troubled sea when it cannot rest, whose waters cast up mire and dirt. There is no peace, saith the Lord, to the wicked." The man who carries a sense of sin in his heart, whose selfishness has injured other lives, whose lust and impurity have defiled the soul, whose dishonesty has accumulated a great mass and weight upon his soul, is inwardly torn to pieces and he knows no peace.

Desperation may come to the child of God as well. The one who has known fellowship with Christ, who has known peace, who has received forgiveness can grieve the Holy Spirit through neglect and willfulness. His fellowship with God can be broken temporarily, and in the far country, the prodigal is miserable. But there is recourse for the sinner, the glorious provision of God in Jesus Christ our Lord. "If we confess our sins He is faithful and just to forgive us our sins and to cleanse us from all unrighteousness" (I John 1:9). When I go to Christ in surrender and lay my guilty life in His hands, when I appeal to the merits of His love and redeeming death I can take from the hand of God the forgiveness of sin and know His peace. This is therapy at the deepest level. Then let us confess to God exactly what we are and how we feel. Let us commit to Him our way and rely upon Him completely.

Let me outline some practical steps on how to get on top of our troubles and master our moods.

The first step is a simple one. Take a piece of paper and write down precisely what is bothering you. Fears and discouragement are like balloons. They can be blown up to large and frightening shapes and sizes but they really don't weigh anything. They are just a lot of air. When you write down the specific things that are bothering you, you deflate them. You bring them closer to their size and discover that about half of your fear is groundless.

When Justice Oliver Wendell Holmes was in a despondent mood, his wife wrote a letter to him and placed it on his desk. She said, "Dear Oliver, You have lived a long time and have seen many troubles most of which never happened. Some of the griefs and the sharpest you have survived, but what torments of grief you have endured from fears of events which never arrived." How futile to carry the burden of things that are not there. Put them down in black and white. Look at them and they will deflate before your eyes.

Another suggestion is to decide that you don't want to worry. You say, "That is silly. Nobody wants to worry or be distressed and discouraged." Wait a minute! Some of you really do. You are indulging your moods. You are cultivating your concerns. You are feeding your fears because this, in a sense, feeds your self-pity. It gives you an opportunity to draw on the sympathy of others and it releases you from certain responsibilities in life. You really hug these things to your heart. You like them! So, another very helpful step is to decide that you don't want these discouragements and fears. Say to yourself, "I want to be God's man—God's woman. I want to walk in His light, know His poise and joy through Jesus Christ. I choose that instead." You may not believe me but just take my word for it. Look your fears over and see how many of them you want and how many you don't want and get rid of them by renouncing them.

Talk your problems over with a wise friend who knows the ways of God. Principally because of pride it is difficult to talk to another person about one's problems. We do not want anyone to know what kind of person we really are. We do not want anyone to know that we are depressed, blue, despondent, and afraid. So we keep these things locked inside and don't tell anyone about them. They just stay there, festering. But the moment we push aside our foolish pride and tell someone exactly what we are, the light of real objective truth is shed upon the situation.

One summer when we lived out in the country, my four-year-old nephew visited us. The night was warm, and the windows were wide open when he was being tucked in bed by his mother. Outside the window, the crickets were in full orchestration and the little boy from the city who had not heard crickets before said, "What makes that noise? His Mother replied, "The crickets are making that noise." "What's a cricket?" he asked. Did you ever try to describe a cricket? It's difficult. The little fellow thought something as big as a cow was making all that noise. In spite of every consoling word his fears were not reduced and he spent a bad night. The next day, I managed to find a cricket in the garden and I showed it to him. I said, "This is a cricket. He makes the noise you heard last night by rubbing his hind legs together. That was hard for him to believe too! But when I finally persuaded him that that insignificant little bug was the thing that was making the noise, his fears vanished. When we take our moods and our feelings out before the eyes of another we see them in their true size. Mushrooms grow in damp, dark corners and they shivel in the sunshine. Fears and moods grow in damp, dark corners. Move them out into the sunshine and watch them shrink.

Another step is to talk things over with God. This should be the first step. Talk to Him in prayer and let Him speak to you through the Bible. The Psalmist testified "The entrance of Thy word giveth light." How true! When we go to the Bible and let the Spirit of God illuminate its truth, light is brought into the darkness. Again the Psalmist cries, "My soul grieveth unto the dust." What a picture! "My soul grieveth unto the dust. Quicken Thou me according to Thy Word." For he knew that the sure word of truth poured into the heart by the Holy Spirit is life-giving. It quickens us up from the dust. Open the Scripture every morning and every evening. Spend time with God. Surrender yourself to the eternal truth of Christ. Listen to what the Lord is saying to you and then talk to Him in prayer.

> Have we trials or temptations?
> Is there trouble anywhere?
> We should never be discouraged.
> Take it to the Lord in prayer.

Yet another step. Decide what you should do about your situation and do it. Write down what you think God wants you to do about this thing and then do it. About fifty percent of our fears and our moods are dispelled by just seeing them in black and white and another forty percent will go as soon as we begin to do something about them. If you cannot think of anything to do, then find somebody who needs help more than you do and endeavor to do something for him. Sitting around brooding over your misfortunes is a bad way to handle your moods. Get busy. Proceed to do what God indicates in your own mind and heart and help others. Get your eyes on the living Lord. Think of the word of the Apostle Paul written to Christians who were in real trouble. "And we know that all things work together for good to them that love God; to them who are the called according to His purpose" (Romans 8:28). "If God be for us who can be against us" (Romans 8:31). "He that spared not His own Son but delivered Him up for us all how shall He not with Him freely give us all things?" (Romans 8.32). "Who shall lay anything to the charge of God's elect?" (Romans 8.33). "Who shall separate us from the love of Christ? Shall tribulation or distress or persecution or famine or nakedness or peril or sword? Nay, in all these things we are more than conquerors through Him that loved us" (Romans 8:35). "For I am persuaded that neither death nor life nor angels nor principalities nor powers, nor things present nor things to come, nor height nor depth nor any other creature shall be able to separate us from the love of God which is in Christ Jesus our Lord" (Romans 8:38,39). If you have trusted Christ as your Saviour and committed your life to Him, nothing can separate you from the love of God— not even your fears. Then start praising God for His grace and goodness. Even if it is mechanical or an act of the will, stand before the Lord your God and praise His glorious Name.

Recently I heard a returned missionary from China. What a bright wonderful witness he had! Prior to World War II he had gone into the interior of China to a lonely difficult field close to the Tibetan Border. As time went by, difficulties and discouragements pressed upon his heart and mind. A friend happened to visit that area, misunderstood something of the circumstances and communicated some distorted truth which hurt the missionary deeply. In addition, from his slender salary he had taken a little sum regularly and placed it in a savings account in the Bank of Hong Kong, where it had accrued to $150.00. When the Japanese took over the Bank of Hong Kong, he had nothing. His health broke and he was flown over the Hump to India. As he was being flown out in fever and weakness, he prayed, "Lord God, see that I get into a good hospital." But instead of that he found himself in a third-rate hospital where he had little care. The doctors came to him, told him to prepare to face the end as they could do nothing more to help him.

He said, "As I lay there I was not afraid to die but I was ashamed to be ushered into the presence of my King, a defeated and discouraged Christian. I prayed that God would meet me. I said, 'Lord, what is the matter?' In my extremity, the words of Scripture began to speak. **In everything** give thanks for this is the will of God concerning you' 'Rejoice in the Lord and again I say, Rejoice'—words written by one who was in prison for Christ's sake. I had even asked God the meaning of absolute surrender and God taught me in that hospital room that absolute surrender is when I thank Him from my heart for everything. I thanked Him for the difficult years in China. I thanked Him for the misrepresentation of friends. I thanked Him that He had stripped me of all financial resources. I thanked Him for the kind of treatment I had received in the hospital. I thanked Him that I was facing death, and as I was praising God He gave me the 'garment of praise for the spirit of heaviness.' He healed my soul and my body. When my wife came to see me that afternoon, I said 'Go back to the hotel room and get by Keswick hymnal. I'm going to sing the praises of God if it is the last thing I do'."

If you want to exchange the spirit of heaviness for the garment of praise, then put on praise like a garment and thank God for everything.

CHAPTER XV

BEING "A HELPER FIT FOR HIM"

Part IV

(Sex is fun—Enjoy it!)

What a fantastic privilege and sacred responsibility is yours today, teacher, to communicate sex from God's point of view! Pray and ask God to enable you to lead this study with un-embarrased freedom of speech. Your *attitude* in leading this study will determine to a large degree the freedom and honesty your class will feel in responding.

Sex is God-given, God-ordained and God-blessed. Because it is *sacred*, only the Christian can know the fullest and deepest meaning of sex. Yet there are *so many* misconceptions and problems and misunderstandings regarding this tremendously important subject among Christians. Pray that God would make the women's preparation of this study and the time you spend in discussion a time of tremendous blessing and enlightenment; a time of honest freedom in sharing; a time of new commitment to Christ and to their husbands.

Teacher, several weeks ago I recommended you order (or purchase from a Chri.tian bookstore locally) Shirley Rice's book, *Physical Unity in Marriage.* I hope you and each woman in your class has her own copy of this book to refer to. She deals with this whole subject in such a loving and thoroughly Christian way and in much more detail than we can cover in this one chapter. Don't miss the blessing!

Another suggestion I want to make is that you encourage the wives to send for Dr. Ed Wheat's tapes mentioned in their book (page 99). These are *not* for group listening—only for a husband and wife.

A. *OBJECT OF THE LESSON*

　　To bring each wife

　　　　1. to see sex from the Biblical perspective

2. to help her determine the causes and find solutions to any problems she is personally experiencing

3. to help each wife experience the ever-increasing joy of giving and receiving in the sexual relationship that God intends.

B. *DISCUSSION QUESTIONS*

1. Why do you think so many women enter into marriage unprepared for the sexual aspect? (Ignorance, wrong teaching, "old wives tales", undue modesty, etc.)

2. What kind of instruction or training would have been of help to you before your marriage to better prepare you for the sexual relationship—or if you *did* receive such help, share with us what was of special benefit to you?

3. Look at Proverbs 5:15-19 and Song of Solomon 7:6-10. How do these passages point out that pleasure is one of the reasons God gave sex? (These and other passages of scripture clearly emphasize that the one flesh relationship does not refer specifically to reproduction, but, rather to sex as a deep personal experience of spiritual and physical pleasure between marriage partners. This pleasure involves the action of the total personality and it can be the most intense height of physical intimacy and the most profound depth of spiritual oneness between a husband and wife.)

4. Do you think women are meant to enjoy sexual intercourse as well as men? (Yes? It is a *good gift* from God (James 1:17) for *both* to enjoy. God would not give it as a good gift for man to enjoy only and intend it to be something not to be enjoyed by woman. His plan is that it be a mutually satisfying experience. Song of Solomon 4 & 5:10-16)

5. Of what significance is the answer to question 1 in your book to a Christian woman's enjoyment of sex? (So many feel it is wrong, sinful, degrading, debased, etc. and not something to be thoroughly enjoyed—

understanding that God gave it as a *good gift* before sin even entered the world is a very *freeing* thought to some women who have been taught it was wrong. The Bible celebrates sex and its proper use and it is very clear that God Himself gave this physical magnetism between the sexes, not only for the propagation of the human race, but also for the expression of this deepest love and oneness between a man and his wife. Satan delights in taking that which is pure and good and corrupting it and misusing it so that people begin to look upon it as being evil in its source. Sex and marriage are of divine origin. Grace perfects them, sin perverts them.)

6. How can sexual intercourse be so right within marriage and so wrong outside the bonds of marriage? What is the biggest argument against pre-marital sex in your opinion? (God commands us not to have premarital sex, and God's laws are for our good not for our hurt. Sex involves the total personality and you cannot become "one flesh" with another and another and another and not have your personality fragmented. God, who made us, understands so well how we need the security of the marriage relationship of one man and one woman to partake in this deepest possible sharing of ourselves with another).

7. Some authorities say more than 50% of the married women claim to be sexually unfulfilled. What do you think are some of the main causes of such sexual problems between married couples? (Tim LaHaye in *How to be Happy though Married* says most discord in this relationship can be attributed to (1) ignorance (2) selfishness (3) fear).

8. Do you agree or disagree with the statement "a woman's greatest sex organ is her mind?" Why?

9. Using I Cor. 7:2-5, let's see if we can find an answer for each problem given in question #6. What other principles did you find from this passage?

10. How is selfishness destructive in the sexual relationship? (Real, *true* pleasure comes only in the total giving of self for the other's pleasure).

11. Of what importance is communication in this area of our lives? e.g. Should you talk to your husband about any problems, likes or dislikes, hang-ups, etc. regarding the sex act? (Yes, it is so important to communicate together as to what brings mutual pleasure, what is not pleasurable, etc.)

12. If a husband seems to be losing his sexual drive, what are some ways a wife can help correct the situation? (Be understanding, recognize business pressures, improve her own appearance and attitude, encourage him to see a doctor to determine if there is a physical cause, encourage and edify him—build him up.)

13. What is your understanding of "foreplay"? Of what importance is it? (Foreplay is that gentle carressing and fondling of the wife's body done by the husband to help raise her sexual desire to the point where they can enjoy a mutually satisfying climax.)

14. What is the place of prayer in achieving and maintaining a good sexual relationship? (Prayer is vital! Prayer can enable a woman to overcome wrong attitudes and long-established thought patterns and see things from God's point of view. We are as dependent on God in this area of our lives as we are in any other.)

C. *SUGGESTIONS FOR CONCLUSION*

1. Perhaps it would be well to close today's session with some honest answers to some valid questions. Let's close our eyes and meditate on these questions:
   a. Am I guilty of defrauding or withholding from my husband sexually?
   b. Am I subjecting him to unnecessary temptations by not adequately meeting his needs?
   c. Am I the "reluctant dragon" always pleading tiredness? or headache? or another more convenient time?

d. Have I been withholding sex—using it as a tool to get my own way?

If any of these things are true, will you bring that matter to God right now in prayer and purpose to cooperate with Him so that He can transform the physical relationship in your marriage into a source of joy and fulfillment for both of you and into an honor to Him.

2. Read the quote on page 98 of their book and remind the ladies this is the *one*, and for most of us the *only*, area of our lives in which we do not have to share our husbands with anyone. We must share so much of their lives with so many others, but God has given us this cherished, deepest expression of love and oneness . . . this time of sublime joy and fulfillment, in which we do not have to share our husbands with any other person! What a privilege and what a cause for gratitude and thanksgiving!

D. *ADDITIONAL SCRIPTURES*

Song of Solomon (especially 1:2, 15; 4; 5:10-16; 7:6-10) Acts 20:35; Phil. 2:3,4; Gen. 18:12-14; I Thess. 4:3-8; Mal. 2:13-15; Prov. 5:15-19

E. *POSSIBLE PROJECTS*

1. Listen to the tapes listed in *The Godly Woman* or in Extra Helps in the Teacher's Guide.

2. Read some of the suggested books

3. Read Song of Solomon and note each word which points out God's desire for us to find pleasure and freedom in wedded sex.

F. *EXTRA HELPS*

Better Is Your Love than Wine by Jean Banyolak and Ingrid Trobisch, Inter-Varsity Press
The Essence of Marriage by J. A. Fritze, Zondervan
Design for Christian Marriage by Dwight Small, Revell

God, Sex and You by Dr. M. O. Vincent, Lippincott
Tape 2298—"Sex Relationship in Marriage"
Tape 2314—"Sex Is God's Idea Part II—How to Enhance
Sexual Response"
Tape 2591—"Sex and Marriage"

CHAPTER XVI

USING THE HOME AS A PLACE OF MINISTRY

Genuine hospitality shown by committed Christians in a decidely Christian home is a powerful and needed witness to the Christian and non-Christian community.

I Peter 4:9 in the Phillips translation exhorts us to "be hospitable without secretly wishing you hadn't got to be!" How many times have we been hospitable—but secretly wished we "hadn't got to be?" In Romans 12:13 in the Living Bible, Paul writes, "When God's children are in need, you be the one to help them out. And get into the habit of inviting guests home for dinner or, if they need lodging, for the night."

So pray, teacher, that this lesson will open the eyes and hearts of the women to ways they can allow God to express Himself and His love to others through the hospitality of their home.

A. *OBJECT OF THE LESSON*

1. To show how God can use a thoroughly Christian home as a center for ministry.

2. To motivate couples to allow God to express His love to others through the hospitality of their home.

B. *DISCUSSION QUESTIONS*

1. Is your home a place to which people come or from which they go? If people (including your husband and children) enjoy your home, why do you think this is true?

2. What are some reasons that might keep us from inviting others into our homes? (selfishness, pride, thinking it is not good enough—or it is too good, don't want to be bothered, etc.) If we *do* invite others in, what could keep this from being "hospitality?" (our attitudes)

3. How would you describe your "neighbor"? (#2 page 100)

4. If you have given hospitality to some godly people what effect do you feel this has had on: (a) you? (b) your mate? (c) your children? (d) your ministry?

5. Do you have any guidelines regarding offering hospitality to strangers?

6. To whom would we not offer hospitality? (#8 page 102) Why?

7. Look up Luke 6:38, II Cor. 9:6, Eccl. 11:1. How do these verses apply to showing hospitality?

8. What new insights did you get in the area of hospitality from the study?

9. What do you think most hinders your own hospitality? (lack of planning, selfishness, not on priority list, business)

10. Share characteristics of the most hospitable couple you know. (generosity, graciousness, servant heart, well organized, love that treats others as they would like to be treated, unselfishness that means sacrifice, mercifulness that shows sympathy, gentleness that speaks softly)

11. Let's look up the following verses and see what attitudes and qualities important to hospitality are found in them:
    a. Matt. 20:26,27—(Servant heart)
    b. I Cor. 13:4-7—(Love)
    c. Col. 3:23—(Wholeheartedness and enthusiasm)
    d. Prov. 11:16—(Gracious)
    e. James 2:1-4—(no respecter of persons)
    f. Prov. 11:24,25—(generosity)
    g. I Peter 4:9 Phillips—(cheerfully without wishing you "hadn't got to")
    (Teacher, ask them to suggest other attitudes and qualities they can think of)

12. What are some thoughts on preparing for real Christian hospitality?

a. *For House Guests? Prepare a place*—prepare bed, room, drawer, and closet space (if available), towels, drinking glass, etc. If possible, add a "homey" touch like a basket of fruit or a fresh flower, etc.

Prepare yourself—Be ready for their arrival. Be dressed, hair combed, etc. Think through on conversation topics. Plan meals ahead of time.

After they arrive—Set aside a time to rest, relax, bathe, nap, be alone, etc. Offer to shop for them or take them shopping if they would like to, offer refreshments, acquaint them with the house, plan things they'd enjoy doing (good to check this with them first—offer several options), RELAX, make them feel at home!

b. *For Dinner Guests*—Plan the menu ahead of time; make sure you have all necessary ingredients; plan time schedule so dinner will be on time and you will have time to freshen up and not be rushed and harried; plan questions or topics for conversation; be ready to welcome and make them feel at home; RELAX!

c. *Guests Just For An Afternoon Or Evening Visit*— Plan to have the house and yourself ready when they arrive; at some point you may wish to offer coffee, hot tea or iced tea, etc. If you plan to serve a dessert or snack make it simple enough so that preparation or serving of it does not require a great deal of your time. Plan conversation topics, etc.

In receiving *any guest* in our home, we should concentrate on *them* (Phil. 2:3,4) not ourselves. Be warm, friendly, gracious, thoughtful, express appreciation for their being there, show love, etc.

13. How can your home be a place of ministry if your husband is not keen on being involved in hospitality? (Ask his permission to have a Bible study or prayer group during the day; have a friend in for coffee; let it be a place of ministry to your children their friends, etc.)

C. SUGGESTIONS FOR CONCLUSION

1. If you did the assignment on page 102 share what positive plans you and your husband have to make your home a more available tool in the hands of God for the blessing of others.

2. Let's spend a few moments in quiet meditation and prayer, asking God to show us some specific person with a need to whom we can extend Christian love and hospitality this week (or this month) e.g. perhaps a foreign student, a senior citizen, someone seldom in a loving home situation, a non-Christian couple, or family, etc.

3. Have a time of conversational prayer with regard to whatever areas of need the Lord has shown them in this matter of using their home as a center of ministry. (Teacher, if you are not acquainted with conversational prayer, it is described in Rosalind Rinker's book, *Prayer, Conversing with God*.)

D. ADDITIONAL SCRIPTURES

I Peter 3:15; I Tim. 3:2; Romans 14:7; Matt. 5:48; Phil. 2:14, 15; Col. 1:9,10 (Phillips)

E. POSSIBLE PROJECTS

1. Invite a couple or individuals you are seeking to help grow spiritually over for a meal or an evening.
2. Memorize and meditate on several choice verses on hospitality.
3. Offer your home for a Bible Study or prayer fellowship.

F. EXTRA HELPS

God's Best Secrets by Andrew Murray
Heaven Help the Home by Howard Hendricks
Tape BSU 120—"The Home as a Center of Worship and
    Ministry"
Tape 1501—"Helping your Husband in his Ministry";
    "Hospitality"

CHAPTER XVII

RESPONSIBILITIES TO OUR CHILDREN

God has placed in our hands the tremendous responsibility—and great privilege—of teaching and training our children for His glory! What a fantastic trust! This requires nothing short of Godly parents totally committed to Him and totally relying on Him!

There are many excellent tapes and books on this subject, Teacher. Some are mentioned on page 109 of the *Godly Woman* study. I would recommend that you avail yourself of some of these in preparation for teaching this lesson. You will find I use some quotes from Shirley Rice's book, *The Christian Home*, I would highly recommend it to you and to your class. She has several very excellent chapters on children. Another good book for parents of teenagers is *Shut Your Generation Gap* by Bill McKee.

Teacher, you may have mothers who feel they have made every possible mistake with their children. Some may be discouraged thinking it's too late for them to find out God's principles for raising children now. So it would be well to remind them that our God is a Redeemer God and He can even use our mistakes for good in the lives of our children. And they can *still* have a profound influence even on their grown children by the sweet fragrance of a Godly life—"The unmistakable 'scent' of Christ, discernable alike to those who are being saved and to those who are heading for death . . . " II Corinthians 2:14 (Phillips). The Christian and the non-Christian should be able to smell the sweet fragrance, the unmistakeable scent of Christ in our lives.

Perhaps you will want to use the following poems at some point in the lesson.

CHILDREN LEARN WHAT THEY LIVE

If a child lives with criticism—
  He learns to condemn,
If a child lives with hostility—
  He learns to fight,

If a child lives with ridicule—
   He learns to be shy,
If a child lives with shame—
   He learns to feel guilty,
If a child lives with tolerance—
   He learns to be patient,
If a child lives with encouragement—
   He learns confidence,
If a child lives with praise—
   He learns to appreciate,
If a child lives with fairness—
   He learns justice,
If a child lives with security—
   He learns to have faith,
If a child lives with approval—
   He learns to like himself,
If a child lives with acceptance and friendship—
   He learns to find love in the world
                              Dorothy Law Nolte

SEND THEM TO BED WITH A KISS

O mothers, so weary, discouraged,
   Worn out with the cares of the day,
You often grow cross and impatient,
   Complain of the noise and the play;
For the day brings so many vexations,
   So many things go amiss;
But mothers, whatever may vex you,
   Send the children to bed with a kiss!

The dear little feet wander often,
   Perhaps from the pathway of right,
The dear little hands find new mischief
   To try you from morning till night;
But think of the desolate mothers
   Who'd give all the world for your bliss,
And, as thanks for your infinite blessings,
   Send the children to bed with a kiss!

For some day their noise will not vex you,
   The silence will hurt you far more;
You will long for their sweet, childish voices,

for a sweet childish face at the door;
And to press a child's face to your bosom,
  You'd give all the world for just this!
For the comfort 'twill bring you in sorrow,
  Send the children to bed with a kiss!

New Orleans Picayune

A. *OBJECT OF THE LESSON*

1. To teach the Biblical principles regarding our responsibility to our children

2. To desire to be Godly parents

3. To begin or continue operating on Biblical principles in raising our children

B. *DISCUSSION QUESTIONS*

1. Share some ways your children have been a spiritual blessing to you.

2. What was the most outstanding principle or insight that you got from the lesson?

3. What has happened in your life that would point out the truth that God gave children because of what they would do for you?

4. In questions 2 and 3 what are some of the parents' responsibilities to their children? Did you find any new insights here?

5. Turn to Luke 2:40 and 52. What four areas of growth in Jesus' life are mentioned here? (Physical, mental or emotional, Spiritual, and social). Do you feel your child is growing in all four of these areas? What attention do you give to training him and aiding him in his growth in each of these areas? Are you giving as much time, thought and training to the spiritual growth as to the other three areas? (Teacher, allow time for discussion between each of these questions).

6. What are the basic things you feel a child needs to grow up into a mature, God-fearing, law-abiding in-

dividual? (Love and discipline . . . *both* are most essential because "Love without discipline is sentiment. Discipline without love is tyranny"—Shirley Rice.)

7. Looking at the ways we love our children, how would you describe a healthy, balanced love? (#4 page 104. Love that fosters independence and maturity; love that holds the child to the highest, demanding the best of him but not expecting more than he is capable of producing; love that encourages, lets him know you are proud of him, expresses confidence—this is mature love.)

8. Looking at the other side, what characterizes a possessive love? (Love that is selfish. A self-love rather than a love for the child makes the child dependent and fosters immaturity. This is immature love.)

9. What advice would you ladies give to a mother who has *already* spoiled her child, but longs to correct the situation? (Teacher, be sure the ladies bring out the need for *consistent* discipline in their comments. The book, *Parents on the Run*, has some excellent thoughts on this.)

10. How do you teach your child to make right choices?

11. Discuss definitions of teach, train, discipline, etc. Did this help you better understand *what* your responsibility is? What are some ways we *teach* our children?

12. How do you think we teach our children to honor us as parents? (We must be worthy of their honor. G. Campbell Morgans says, "The surest way to insure that children shall honor parents is for the parents to live the life before them that reflects the glory and the grace of God".)

13. What ways of making your child secure impressed you the most, or was your area of greatest need?

14. What are some practical ways to build security in the lives of our children?

15. What are some guidelines for discipline you follow with your children?

16. What principle of discipline or verse impressed you the most? Which one do you have the most difficulty following? Why?

17. What are some reasons we don't discipline? What can we do about it with God's help?

18. How do you feel about your child—whom you are seeking to raise according to Christian principles—playing with a neighbor's child whose language and conduct is not in accord with these principles . . . especially if it is a neighbor you are seeking to witness to, or if this is the only playmate your child has? (Shirley Rice in *The Christian Home* gives this advice: "The only way we can solve this problem is to lay a good foundation to relate the child rightly to God and to Christ, to know the source of power they have in Him, and to be happy about this power and about His attitude and interest in children. Teach them to turn to God for help at home, or at play, or at school. Encourage them to look to the One who can help them. We don't want to rear houseplants—our children will meet evil. I think we should arrange so that situations are not too bad. Strengthen them in their relationship to God, and they will have the help they need when they must go apart from their purely Christian environment".)

19. Share what you consider one strength and one weakness you have as a parent.

20. In what way do you fail most to encourage your children?

21. What do you feel the mother contributes to the atmosphere of the home? (Although the father is the head of the home, the mother sets the general atmosphere of the home. Dr. Norman Harrison likens the father to the rim of the wheel—coming as a protective cushion between the family and the world . . . taking the jolts and hardships for his family. Dr. Harrison likens the mother to the hub of the wheel—Everything in the home revolves around her. As

the hub goes, so goes the wheel. If the hub is off center, the whole wheel is thrown off balance.)

C. *SUGGESTIONS FOR CONCLUSION*

1. Look over the ways of encouragement (Page 107) and pick one to work on this week. Write it down now. Determine a specific way you could improve in that area. Write it down, share it with the class. Commit it to God in prayer as we close and tell God you purpose to cooperate with Him to be consistent in encouragement and in discipline this week.

2. Go over the list of Practical Helps (page 108-109). Ask each woman to choose one thing from each section—(a) the life of the parent (b) encouragement (c) discipline or training—to pray for every day this week and work on. Encourage them to select another one from each section next week, and the next week, etc., to pray over and work on.

D. *ADDITIONAL SCRIPTURE*

Ps. 128 (LB); John 10:28; Lam. 3:27; Col. 3:21; Prov. 6:20; Hosea 6:1; Deut. 5:29; Heb. 10:24,25; Ps. 32:8-9; Gen. 18:19; I Sam. 1:11,27; Titus 1:8; Prov. 17:27,28; Prov. 22:15; Prov. 20:30

E. *POSSIBLE PROJECTS*

1. Give each woman one or two chapters from a book to read, or a tape to listen to; then give a 5-10 minute report on it. For instance, you could assign:
   a. *Parents on the Run*—Chapters 6 and 7
   b. *The Christian Family*—Pages 63-74
   c. *Dare to Discipline*—Pages 15-49 one person, Pages 63-90 another person
   d. *Heaven Help the Home*—Chapter 4
   e. Howard Hendrick's tapes—Childrearing I and II and III (Tape 1150 AB, 1151 AB, & 1152 AB)

2. Set aside a regular time weekly to do something that each child likes to do.

3. Underline verses with your children each week that will build character and have them start a notebook of these verses.
4. From the list of weaknesses and strengths, work this week on building up weaknesses and continue working on strengths.
5. Ask children what discipline means to them. Go through Proverbs with them and point out principles of discipline in Proverbs.
6. Begin to have a time of family prayer together before putting the children to bed each night.

F. *EXTRA HELPS*

Hide or Seek by James Dobson, Tyndale House
Reconstruction of Family Life by E. Trueblood
The Marriage Affair by J. A. Peterson (Chapter 6)
Tape 1819—"Creative Motherhood"
Tape 1067—"Training Children Ages 7-12"
Tape 969, 970—"God's Plan for Your Child; The Place of Prayer in Child Training"

Appendix

Appendix

Appendix

Contents

CHAPTER I
WHY BIBLE STUDY?

MANY PEOPLE THROUGHOUT THE WORLD TODAY ARE BIBLICALLY IGNORANT. Many claim not to believe the Bible, although they have never read it. The Bible claims some amazing things for itself, among which are: it is a guide; through it God brings health, growth, peace, understanding, salvation, and protection, just to mention a few. Since God can do these things and many more through the Bible, men desperately need to know what God has to say in His Word. Men who are confused and bewildered by their own lives and the world around them, when exposed to the powerful Word of God, find answers to their deepest longings and needs. As Bible discussion leaders, we have the privilege of being part of God's plan for reaching, teaching, and training men and women to accomplish His perfect will for their lives.

CHAPTER II
WHY A SMALL GROUP?

The small group idea is not new. Almost two thousand years ago, the followers of Jesus Christ drew together in small groups to continue in the Word, prayer, fellowship with one another, and seeking for a greater outreach in the community.[1] The book of Acts records the impact and vitality of these small groups and their experience around the person of Christ. One man with a genuine desire and hunger for the Lord is enough to spark and inflame a group. One group, in turn, is enough to ignite a dormitory, military barracks, business office, neighborhood or church. And motivated, inflamed men and women are enough to penetrate and saturate a community with Christ-centered disciples. Initially, the real question is not one of quantity, but quality. As Jonathan said to his armor-bearer, "Perhaps the Lord will work for us, for the Lord is not restrained, save by many or by few."[2]

What ingredients will make a group successful? Here is an almost sure-fire recipe:

START with one person with a desire for the Lord, SIFT in a few other eager Christians, plus some others who want to meet Jesus, or know Him better. BLEND in a balanced, interesting course of study, ADD a cup of prayer and another cup of preparation. STIR in a tablespoon of common sense, DROP in a pinch of humor. SKIM off the religious jargon, the do's and don'ts, the over-emotionalism. SEASON with generous portions of acceptance, genuine, personal interest and love. REMOVE preachiness, self-effort and the holier-than-thou attitude. ALLOW the influence of the Holy Spirit to lift hearts to worshipping the Lord Jesus Christ Himself. Follow this recipe of leading group discussions, and they will almost never burn, over-bake, sour, or fall flat.

There are some specific values in meeting together as a group:

1. *Fellowship*

"Two are better than one; because they have a good

---

[1] Acts 2:42
[2] I Samuel 14:6b

reward for their labour. For if they fall, the one will lift up his fellow: but woe to him that is alone when he falleth; for he hath not another to help him."[3] We need each other— God has made us that way. "Iron sharpeneth iron; so a man sharpeneth the countenance of his friend."[4]

2. *The interactions of a group produce faster learning.*

There is more to learning than listening. We learn to do by doing. By meeting each other in small groups we benefit from group dynamics in:

—finding what the Bible has to say.
—having open discussion
—having a meaningful sharing of our lives
—learning to pray together
—motivating us to outreach
—there will be time for each to contribute
—regular study will be encouraged.
—there will be better stimulation of personal application
—each will be more free to share.
—All will get to know the others well.
There are hindrances to every one of these benefits:

Finding what the Bible has to say—Laziness, preconceived ideas, unwillingness to accept it as the authentic and authoritative Word of God.

Having open Discussion—Domineering leader. Leader who is an authority figure or who is afraid of revealing his lack of knowledge.

Having a meaningful sharing of our lives—Having an honest sharing life is a difficult thing in the Christian context today. We are afraid to be honest with each other. Some of the fears are well-founded. Some are afraid they will be judged and rejected. Others, that they will be gossipped about. Still others, that people will not understand their problems. Yet others, that they may simply get a pat answer from the Bible instead of understanding and counsel. Whatever the cause for this faking each other out, it is one of

[3] Ecclesiastes 4:9,10
[4] Proverbs 27:17

the means which has effectively blocked the full flow of God's power by His Spirit into many groups.

Learning to pray together. Some people are afraid of the sound of their own voices. We learn to swim by getting into the water. We learn to pray by praying. Some practical suggestions can be found under the heading, "The Elements of an Effective Bible Discussion Group." These suggestions will enable you to help the group members to experience the joy of praying together.

Motivating us to outreach. Many Christians either want to reach out to a lost and dying world but don't know how, or are afraid to try. The Bible discussion group can be helpful in overcoming these problems by preparing the members to share their own personal experience with Christ in a meaningful way, equipping them to present the facts of the Gospel and by providing settings in which outreach may occur most naturally. Some means available for such help are:

(1.) Personal calling on friends, neighbors, or associates with another group member.

(2.) Evangelistic coffees or teas.

(3.) Andrew dinners. Committed couples bringing uncommitted couples together for an evening of food and fellowship.

(4.) As a group inviting friends to join you at a crusade, evangelistic film showing, special speaker, etc.

(5.) Group members organizing and leading evangelistic studies. Groups without outreach soon become ingrown and die.

3. *Pressure to prepare.*
Most of us are lazy and won't do an effective job of preparing in Bible discussion if we do not have the pressure of a group.

4. *Application and a way to check up on our applications.* God is not nearly as interested in *teaching* us something as He is

in *making* us something. He is more interested in what we *are*[5] than what we *do*.

5. *It will help us learn how to lead a group ourselves.*

CHAPTER III.

THE TYPES OF BIBLE STUDY

1. *Mama-Bird Study.*

   This is one where the mama bird (teacher) goes to the Bible, digs out all of the little goodies and drops them into the open, waiting, and expectant mouths of the members of the group. This is the least effective type of study because it has the least retention and effect upon the personal lives of those who attend.

2. *Share Your Ignorance.*

   This is when a group decides that they will get together for Bible study and upon arriving they decide to look at the second chapter of Luke, for instance, and then share their ignorance on the subject with no prior preparation.

3. *Question and Answer.*

   There is a sense in which this is predigested food but is an excellent study for teaching basic Bible doctrine and truth.

4. *Inductive.*

   This is where each member of the group goes to a portion of the Word of God and discovers the facts that are there, tries to understand what they mean, makes an application to his own life with the group coming together simply to discuss what they have found in personal study.

CHAPTER IV.

THE DISCUSSION GROUP ITSELF

A discussion group is not a lecture or a conversation between two opinionated people. The United States Post Office has a definition of a group that readily applies to the definition of the Bible study discussion group:

"A group of capable people put together by design
   working with shared concern
      toward meaningful objectives
         according to a plan
            at high levels of performance
               within a framework of policies
                  (and a relationship to God and each other—
                  editor's note)
                     to which all are committed."

Ideally, group Bible discussions are the cooperative search for the solution to a problem, the type of interaction where decisions are made, and real learning takes place. This demands a mutual expression of interest in the subjects under study by the members of the group. The leader asks a question, and waits for the group to respond. He can then ask what the others find, or what facts did someone else discover? Again, looking around the whole group, waiting for anyone to speak. His job is that of a traffic policeman or a band director, bringing the members in or allowing them to contribute as the discussion continues. The leader should not do all of the talking, or even most of it. The leader does not have to possess all of the answers or be the authority figure. When the discussion group is functioning properly, the leader will no longer be the focus of the group. Replies will not be directed to the leader, but soon they will begin to reply and discuss among themselves. Then the discussion becomes group-centered.

CHAPTER V.

THE ELEMENTS OF AN EFFECTIVE
BIBLE DISCUSSION GROUP

The elements of an effective Bible discussion group should be:

1. A consistent study and personal application of the Word of God.

2. Prayer.

3. An honest sharing of the life.

4. Outreach.

Learning to pray together can be one of the richest experiences of the discussion group, many of whom have never prayed aloud in the presence of one another. One suggestion for "easing" one into praying before others without causing them embarrassment or fear is to have a time of group prayer with each one taking his turn. Suggest that prayers be sentence prayers, thanking God for one specific thing. Explain that if a person does not want to formulate a prayer of his own, when it comes his turn, simply to say, "Thank You, Lord" which will indicate to the next person that he may begin to pray.

After having experienced sentence prayers of thanksgiving together, another type of prayer is conversational prayer. It is an easy thing to learn how to pray together. The honest sharing of the application will naturally lead to an outpouring of confession, praise, and petition, and heart-felt prayer at the end of the discussion. To do this, a group needs to concentrate on saying things that they really mean. Learning how to say exactly what they think or feel at the moment requires honesty and openness with the Lord and to one another. The objective is to learn to pray conversationally about common needs, in sentence prayers in order to give all the opportunity to take part. As a leader, you might begin, for instance, by sharing your heart with the Lord in the first person singular. (I, me, my, instead of we, us, or they). As you begin, and then continue, hopefully, another person in the group will feel led to share his heart on the same subject. He is simply carrying on the same prayer of the first person with hardly a break in thought. To encourage the group to stick to one topic at a time, you, as the leader should change the subject the first few times until the group catches on to the process. The tendency is to want to change the subject too soon. You will want to keep your prayers to one or two sentences so as not to monopolize the prayer time and to set the example for the next person. You should let the group then volunteer to pray but not force them. This can be accomplished, naturally, by going around the circle.

Here are some simple rules for conversational prayer to keep in mind.

1. Pray briefly so that everyone has the opportunity to pray several times.

2. Pray loudly so that everyone can hear.

3. Pray topically, so that everyone has the opportunity to pray about the same subject.

4. Pray specifically so that everyone zeroes in on a particular request.

5. Pray persistently so that everyone present sees that the group really means business.

Another interesting change of prayer is to ask each member of the group to pray for the person on their right after all the applications have been shared. This can be a very rich time indeed. Yet another idea is bidding prayer. In bidding prayer, you, as the leader, have decided on a number of things which the group could or should pray about, and will ask, "Who will pray about this?" When someone has prayed about that particular topic, then introduce another topic. This also can be a meaningful time of group prayer.

CHAPTER VI.

HOW TO START

1. *Recruit people for the group.*
   a. Decide on the target group
   b. Test their interest

2. *Decide on the materials to be used.*

3. *Keep it small.* We should grow in the business instead of going in the business.

4. *Decide on a place and time.*

5. *Decide on the over-all length of the study.*
   (Six weeks, twelve weeks, etc.) Bible discussion groups should always have an ending time. No group should form to go from now until Jesus comes.

6. *Decide on the length of time to be invested* when the group meets. (One hour. 1½ hours, 2 hours, etc.)

7. *Some do's and don'ts of inviting people:*

DO	*DON'T*
Invite people who have common interests and who contribute toward better understanding and communication.	Pressure people. Eager people are the best students.
Be positive, optimistic, and enthusiastic about the study.	Have more than you can handle. Ten is the maximum number I have found practical with which to start.
Ask people to commit themselves to come each week for the specified course of study and to do the necessary preparation.	Be discouraged if only one person is willing to meet with you. God is intensely interested in the individual.

8. *Set the Stage.*
   a. Prepare a comfortable place.
   A home setting is a very relaxed and comfortable place to hold a Bible discussion group.

b. Insure proper ventilation. People being too hot or cold limits their learning ability.

c. Be sure that you have proper lighting.

d. Plan the seating ahead of time. (A semi-circle with the leader in the middle or around the table, et cetera)

e. Make sure everyone has a Bible. In a new group it may be advisable to buy an inexpensive new copy of the same translation by the same printer for each person in the study. That way, instead of looking for the verses by books, chapter and verse, you can look for them by the page number which will keep those who are not very familiar with the Bible from being embarrassed.

f. Prepare against disturbances ahead of time. Telephone, television, doorbell, pets, children, et cetera.

g. Have a good clock clearly visible.

9. *Control the size of the group.*

An ideal group would be not less than four nor more than 10 people. If a group grows too large all the values of being a small group tend to disappear. Fellowship becomes less intimate. Personal involvement diminishes. Stimulation to prepare and the opportunity to share application decreases. The atmosphere becomes less of a group of close friends and more of a committee meeting.

On the other hand, in a small group:

1. Each member counts and knows it. He will be missed if absent.

2. Most homes or rooms can accommodate a small group.

3. More people are willing to lead a small group than a large one, and thus have the opportunity to grow in spiritual leadership.

Sometimes it is helpful to have a group covenant. Because a flimsy, purposeless, undisciplined group works worse than no group at all, it will drive away, rather than attract.

The covenant should look something like this:

1. The supreme authority is to be the Word of God. I am willing to accept this as a rule for the discussion group.

2. The attendance at the meetings will be priority during the duration of the study. I pledge myself to be there for

(?) weeks unless providentially hindered. If I cannot
come, I will let someone know.

3. I will prepare my assignments in advance or not participate in the discussion. I will attend but only audit the
sessions.

4. I will maintain a daily devotional time.

5. I will hold in confidence those things which are shared
in the group. I will not gossip about other members of
the group.

6. I will pray daily as God gives grace for the other people
in my group.

7. I will seek to relate my faith to the world outside, and to
share what I have learned with others.

10. *The First Meeting.*

It is important that people get to know each other if they
are to be an effective part of the Bible discussion group. At
the first meeting you might suggest that they give their
name, where they are from, something about the work they
do and their family. Another good way to introduce people
is to ask them to answer three questions and give them five
minutes within which to do it.

Question #1:   What is the first thing you remember?

       #2:   What people or events have made you
what you are today?

       #3:   What is the happiest moment of your life
that you can remember?

Another way of getting a group introduced to each other
is to use what is called the Quaker dialogue. The questions
are as follows:

Question #1:   Where did you live between the ages of
9 and 13?

       #2:   How did you heat your home during those
years?

#3:   What room in your house (or personal thing was the center of emotional warmth to you during those years?

#4:   When did you first come to realize that God was something more than an idea? (In asking this last question you may explain that you are not looking for their conversion experience, but simply when their own consciousness of God came about and the circumstances which surrounded it.)

In using the Quaker dialogue, you first, as a leader, should answer each of the questions in order to give other members of the group an example of how you intend for them to be answered. On the first three questions you can go around the circle in the group. On the fourth question the answer should be optional.

Anything which can transform them from a number of individuals into a group will be helpful at the outset. Sometimes this can be accomplished through humor, other times by singing, but the necessity of welding the group together is real.

11. *The Discussion Group Leader.*

A. The discussion group leader's responsibilities:

1. To tell the group *WHY* Bible discussion is important to this particular group at this time. As a group leader, you need to be properly and effectively motivated. Your enthusiasm in goal setting will spur the group on to achievement.

2. To show the group *HOW*. Example is the best way to teach. You must have a workable study plan that you are personally using so that you can show them how and what to do.

3. To get the group started. Many people are just waiting for something to do and for someone to show them how. You can provide the incentive for getting started by having a plan, getting them the materials and requiring a fulfilled assignment.

4. To keep the group going. Having a regular weekly meeting to attend and prepare for, is the best way of helping people regularly to do Bible study. Requiring a completed assignment that you will be discussing the following week will encourage them, motivate them and challenge them to be prepared.

B. As the leader, you need:

1. To know well the passage to be studied. It will take a little extra time to dig a little deeper and to look more closely at the verses being studied. Be sure to know and understand the context. But there is no substitute for diligent preparation and prayer. Don't be sidetracked from the priority of your own intensity of study. When you stop studying you stop leading effectively.

2. To be excited about the discoveries of group members. Often a Bible discussion leader will get excited about what he himself is discovering from the text of the scripture. He acknowledges what others find with a nod of the head, an appreciating remark, or a further question. But, when he fails to get excited about new truths the group members are discovering, he demotivates them. Because you have previously discovered a truth that someone has just now discovered, don't quench his search for new truth by your superior attitude. Get excited about what others are excited about—and show it!

3. To use your sense of humor. Spontaneity and freedom are important areas to be developed in the life of the leader. Humor that is well placed, well timed, appropriate, and in the context of what is being studied, will sustain interest in the study. You must develop your own style of humor and not try to imitate another's style.

4. To be enthusiastic. You need not be the one who comes up with the best discoveries, interpretations, or applications. Neither do you need to be the one who uncovers the most revealing background material,

character sketches, or facts. You should, however, be thusiasm as you prepare for the discussion and as you long. Pray that your discussion will be one they will never forget. Ask God to give you a spirit of enthusiasm as you prepare for the discussion and as you lead it. Your attitude will help determine the attitude of each member in your group.

5. To use creative illustrations and visualizations. Eye-catchers and ear-catchers captivate interest. Simple little illustrations communicate more readily than complex ones—a picture, a drawing, a story, or personal illustration, can provide your group members with a point of identification with you. Encourage the participants in the group to share their own creativity.

6. To put the group to work. Those who consistently and enthusiastically complete the study, apply the Word of God and participate in the discussion, will want to get involved in helping others to do the same. Putting them to work leading other discussion groups or involving them in personal evangelism, visitation programs, Sunday School classes, conferences, personal follow-up and counselling will help them to reproduce Christ-centered lives in the lives of others. This is called making disciples.

7. To become personally involved with the members of the group. "Love never fails."[6] People desperately need someone to care whether they sink or swim spiritually. As a leader you can make all of the mistakes in the book, but if you genuinely care, people will continue to come and respond to your leadership. The apostle Paul is an excellent example of someone who really cared. "But we were gentle among you, even as a nurse cherisheth her children. So being affectionately desirous of you, we were willing to have imparted unto you, not the gospel of God only, but also our own soul, because ye were dear unto us."[7]

---

[6] I Corinthians 13:8
[7] I Thessalonians 2:7,8

Then he said, "I pray that you will live good lives, not because that will be a feather in our caps, proving that what we teach is right; no, for we want you to do right even if we ourselves are despised." And, "We are glad to be weak and despised if you are really strong. Our greatest wish and prayer is that you will become mature Christians."[8]

a. *Learn to Listen.* Listening to someone is one of the highest compliments that you can pay them.

    (1) (Listen attentively).

        Use your eyes to look at a person. Don't glance off because he doesn't seem eager to respond. Be observant of what people say and use their statements to formulate other questions. It was said that President Kennedy made you think that he had nothing else to do except ask you questions and listen, with extraordinary concentration to your answer. You knew that for the time being he had blotted out both the past and the future.

    (2) (Be prepared to wait for an answer).

        Waiting demonstrates your real interest and concern. Give a person time to think. You may want to re-state the question. Also be attentive to second thoughts. Often a person will think of more to say on an issue or be able to clarify his position after he makes his first statement. It is common for people to think of what they should have said. If you sense this, be alert enough to come back for more information. "Do you have any more thoughts on that?" or, "Would you like to add anything else?"

b. *Pray.* One of the biggest ministries that you will have is praying for your group members. Much more will happen in their lives throughout the week if you conscientiously and consciously con-

---

[8] II Corinthians 13:7 and 9 (Living Bible)

centrate on praying for their specific, individual needs. Bring these things boldly before the throne of grace. The Lord will honor this heart-felt conviction and concern.

c. *Live what you teach.* The example of your life will speak more loudly than all the high advice you can give. Different members may not always believe what you say, but they cannot help but believe what you are.

CHAPTER VII.

PREPARING FOR THE DISCUSSION

As a discussion group leader, you need to do at least three things in the way of specific preparation prior to the group meeting. You need to:

determine your objective,

divide the lesson into manageable segments,

prepare a lesson plan.

1. *Objectives.* A good discussion group leader will begin with and objective clearly in mind. "He who aims at nothing hits it every time". So be sure you have an objective in mind. Don't fall into the trap of flying by the seat of your pants, hoping that everything will work out. An objective is a brief statement which summarizes what you want from the group meeting. Ask yourself, "What do I want the group to *know, feel,* and *do* by the time the discussion is completed." A clear objective will help you do four things.

   a. It will help tell you where you are heading with the discussion and give you direction for your questions.

   b. It will help you evaluate progress at any point during the discussion. After this evaluation you can make any adjustments.

   c. It will allow you to make decisions along the way as to what to discuss. If a tangent issue arises, you can direct the group back to the main goal and temporarily table the tangent. But remember the tangent and deal with it later, perhaps in private.

   d. It will help you evaluate how effective the time has been.

2. *Divide the lesson into manageable segments.*

   In question and answer studies or in studying portions of the Word of God you will find that the writers had certain basic ideas in mind which they were trying to put across. When you have discovered how much of the lesson a major idea covers, then you are prepared to lead the discussion on that portion. Sometimes, chapters cannot be broken down into neat packages but it's well worth the effort to attempt to determine what these logical divisions are in order to make the discussion more meaningful.

3. *The Lesson Plan.*

The lesson plan will be helpful in assuring that you accomplish your objective, cover the material that you need to cover, and that you do not spend too much time on any one particular point. The following is an example of a suggested lesson plan.

LESSON PLAN

Chapter to be discussed   One

Time allowed for discussion   One hour

Date of discussion   6/2/75

Place of discussion   Dining Room table

Objective. (What do I want the group to know, feel, and do?)

To know: To be sure each one knows Jesus Christ personally and is assured of it.

To feel: assured of their salvation—based on the *facts* of God's Word.

To do: To be able to clearly share the gospel with another.

   I.   Introduction and Prayer. (10 minutes)

  II. Discussion

      A. FIRST DIVISION: Main Truth, Theme, or Concept
         Who Jesus Christ is
         Time Allotted   10 minutes

         LEADING QUESTIONS:

         1. What divine attribute of Jesus means the most to you?

         2. What human characteristic of Jesus means the most to you??

         3. What does Jesus have to do with the operating of the natural laws today?

B. SECOND DIVISION: Main Truth, Theme, or Concept
What Jesus did

Time Allotted   10 minutes

LEADING QUESTIONS:
1. Is conversion the completion of salvation?

2. Luke 19:10 says "Jesus came to seek and to save the lost." Who are the lost?
3. How does Jesus "seek the lost"? How does He save them?

C. THIRD DIVISION: Main Truth, Theme, or Concept
What the Life, death, and resurrection of Jesus means.
Time Allotted   15 minutes

LEADING QUESTIONS:

1. Why is the resurrection important to genuine Christianity?

2. In your opinion what is a Christian? How does one become one?

3. What is repentence? How important is this to conversion?

(Some lessons may have more or less divisions, depending on the number of main themes)

III.   CONCLUSION. Summary and prayer. (10 minutes)

IV.   Assignment for next week session. (5 minutes)

As you begin or continue leading Bible discussion groups don't fall into the three major traps of discussion leaders.

1. *Comparing yourself to others.* The Bible warns us against doing this. "Not that we venture to class or compare ourselves with some of those who commend themselves. But when they measure themselves by one another, and compare themselves with one another, they are without understanding."[9] Comparison is the denial of God's special place for

_____
[9] II Cor. 10:12

you. Each individual is unique, and the Lord has given each special abilities that are needed if the body of Christ is to function properly.

2. *Giving up.*

Don't throw in the towel. There is a need to stick with the goal to completion. "Better is the end of a thing than the beginning thereof."[10] Be a finisher. Everybody has to start where they are with what they have and do what they can. *"Never give up"* is the best policy to follow in leading discussion groups.

3. *Discouragement.*

Discouragement is spiritual anemia. Our God is the God of encouragement. And you can always trace discouragement to Satan. Don't get discouraged, but continue to "press toward the mark for the high calling of God in Christ Jesus."[11] He will encourage you with blessings from His Word. "Don't be impatient for the Lord to act. Keep traveling steadily along His pathway and in due season He will honor you with every blessing."[12]
There are three main ways you can discourage a discussion group:

a. *Rushing the lesson.* If you have too much material to cover and are rushed, you will transfer your tension to the group and they, in turn, will get frustrated. Most groups prefer less to swallow, and less to chew on, than gulping down big bites. Choose the most crucial material and skip the rest.

b. *Skipping around the text.* Sometimes you may be tempted to skip around the Bible using cross-references, to interpret and explain obscure passages. If you do this too much, you will lose your group in page turning and thought-following. It is best to stick within a chapter

---

10 Ecc. 7:8
11 Philippians 3:14
12 Psalm 37:34 (Living Bible)

and uncover what it has to say about a particular subject before moving outside.

c. *Monopolizing with monologues.* It is so easy to move into spontaneous sermonizing and sharing your brilliant observations and ideas instead of getting into the Bible and helping the group discover the meaning. People are basically hungry to know what the Bible is saying and not necessarily what you are saying. Be sure that you give your discussion group first crack at the text before you get turned on. Keep your finger close to your own "OFF" button.

Remember that we are teaching people and not lessons. Don't be bound by the materials, but meet the needs of the people in your group.

CHAPTER VIII.

GOALS OF BIBLE STUDY

The three basic goals of Bible study are:
DISCOVERY—What does it say?
UNDERSTANDING—What does it mean?
APPLICATION—What does it mean to me?

In your own study and in the study time of the group, these principles should be taught and followed:

1. *Discovery.* Discovery can be defined as the act of seeing and taking notice of things as they really are—the art of awareness. It answers the questions, "What does it say?" Accurate discovery is essential to accurate understanding and application. Adequate discovery depends upon root attitudes. The basic attitudes are openness of mind and openness of life. Too often, people come to Bible study with preconceived notions. Their attitude is "Don't confuse me with the facts. My mind is made up." The wise man is always open to new ideas. In fact, he looks for them.[13]

The person who doesn't have an open life won't see certain things. Whenever we guard some area of our life, we hinder our understanding. A man who is not open to being changed in his marriage won't see anything that would indicate that a change should occur. The woman who won't admit to vanity in her life won't see it described in the scriptures. There are three steps to making good discoveries.

PRAYER
READING
RECORDING

PRAYER is an act of the will and an acknowledgement before God that you are dependent upon the Lord and His Spirit to reveal truth to you. The psalmist prays, "Open thou mine eyes, that I may behold wondrous things out of thy law."[14] Paul continually prays in his letters that the Spirit would open the eyes of understanding to his converts.[15]

---

[13]Proverbs 18:15 (Living Bible)
[14] Psalm 119:18
[15] Ephesians 1:17,18

READING must involve the attitudes of diligence, purpose, thoughtfulness, and inquiry. Reading is not a lazy man's art. Chewing over and assimilating the Bible, meditating until it filters down and jogs the mind and heart requires quality time. When you study you *read for the message, not for the mileage.*

RECORD what you discover. As you write it down, it will force you to clarify your thoughts. You may feel you can't write down everything. The more you can, the more help it will be. If you don't have a good study Bible, try to get one. In it, you can underline important words, write in the margins, and use arrows to connect associated terms.

Often the first step in making a discovery is defining words and phrases. Without the meaning of words there is no possibility of communication or understanding. If you do not have both a good regular dictionary and a Bible dictionary, get them. They are the best possible reference books for Bible study. *Unger's Bible Dictionary* and *New Bible Dictionary* are two suggested helps. *Haley's Bible Handbook* and *Unger's Bible Handbook* will also help.

2. *Understanding.* We assume that the Bible is literal. That is, the Bible *means* what it says. However, there is often more than one definition to a word. Understanding means finding which definition the writer had in mind when he wrote the words. Here are some of the questions which will help you in gaining good understanding.

WHO—	Who are the personalities involved?
WHAT—	What ideas were being conveyed, and what results were expected or gained?
WHERE—	What was the geography? Where did it happen?
WHEN—	What was the time element involved? When did it really take place?
WHY—	Purpose. What was the reason for which it was written?
WHEREFORE—	Application. What did the writer expect to happen as the result of what he wrote?
HOW—	Implementation, method. What plan did the writer have for seeing that his objectives were reached?

There are times when we cannot come to clear conclusions. At this point we must acknowledge the possibilities without being dogmatic. Real understanding is not finding some mysterious hidden meaning through the use of allegorical or symbolic words. The Bible does use some allegories, and symbols but there are usually very easily identified.

You will also want to use the rest of your Bible as a commentary on the particular passage you are studying. The basic approach to the scriptures is dictated by the scriptures themselves. The Bible is its own best commentary. Use cross-references in your study.

3. *Application.*

Since God is more interested in what we are than what we do, application is the most important part of Bible study. It means putting the Word of God into practice, stating the problem and attacking it head-on, recognizing the voice of the Lord, and responding accordingly.

The benefit of Bible study is not the method, the technique, or the diligent efforts of deciphering the text. The benefit is in obeying the voice of the Lord, taking what He says and putting it into practice. Application doesn't happen by chance or by osmosis. Application is by intent. The starting of application is a healthy and immediate response to the truth. A rejection of truth is the result of unbelief and disobedience. The response should be trust, obedience, praise, and thanksgiving. An unwillingness to apply the scriptures personally may tend to develop an intellectual knowledge with spiritual insensitivity to the Lord, and to people.

Our response is always to God and not to a rulebook. Our response is to be motivated by love . . . the goal is to respond to Him at the point where we meet Him in the word. Our ultimate goal is the pursuit of God, pleasing Him in every area of our lives, getting to know Him better and better. Our depth with God can be measured by our obedience to Him and by the depth of our relationship with other people. Shallow relationships with other people indicate a shallow relationship with God.

HOW TO MAKE A PERSONAL
APPLICATION FROM BIBLE STUDY

1. *What impresses me most?*

   (Generally, as you study a subject or a portion, God by His Spirit will lay some particular aspect on your heart. Pray that God will open your eyes to a specific application. Ask Him what He wants you to do about it.)

2. *Where do I fall short in this?*

   (When God speaks to you about a particular aspect of the study, write out the way in which you fall short in this area. Use personal singular pronouns—I, me, my, mine, etc. An application should be *personal, practical,* and *possible.* It should be concerned with a truth which may be translated into daily life and should be clearly stated. The application may deal with your relationship to God or your relationship to man. It should result in personal spiritual enrichment and uplifting by deepening your relationship to the Lord, or should improve your relationship to fellow Christians or those outside of Christ.)

3. *What do I intend to do about it with God's help?*

   (Write out your intentions as a definite action that you will take now to correct the weakness, build the needed quality into your life, strengthen the understanding, etc.) This action may be memorizing a verse on the subject, or making a special study on it, or praying daily about the need. It may be writing a letter of apology, righting some harm done, et cetera. Whatever the action—be specific. Always realize that unless God helps you, real lasting application is impossible.

   We need to ask our discussion group members to make personal applications. Two primary questions must be in the heart of every believer before he tackles the text of any scripture. "Do I have a desire to know God's Word?" and "Do I have a desire to do God's Word?" If either of these questions triggers a negative response, stop the boat, because here's where the Bible student has jumped overboard heading for the falls. The Bible was never given to satisfy men's curiosity, but to change and redirect their lives. God has given His Word in order to reveal Himself and to cause a response in our lives to Him and His principles of living as found in the Bible. The following are seven tendencies or traps that keep us from applying the Word of God properly:

1. The human heart resists change. It always is costly to the pride to stop, change gears, and move in a different direction. We tend to write it off by saying, "I can't possibly do that" or "The Bible is too complex for me to understand" or "Besides, I'm doing okay now."

2. An unwillingness to admit our faults. There is a lack of understanding as to what application really means. The opposite of understanding is not ignorance. In the Christian faith the opposite of understanding is disobedience. To know and not do is not to know at all.

3. There is pressure from society to conform to relative standards and not to the absolute standards of God's authoritative Word. Some say "That's all right, everybody's doing it", or "If I applied that to my life, it would cause me a lot of difficulty at home and at work."

4. There is a tendency to apply the Word of God in areas where I'm already using it. Therefore I redefine sin to fit my model of life and avoid a confrontation with truth that steps on my toes. This can be seen in my attempt to draw up a list of the filthy five, nasty nine and the dirty dozen—a compilation of things I NEVER do.

5. There is a tendency to substitute interpretation for application. This can be seen by too much concern for "How many toes are on the beast of Revelation?" rather than living a holy life in the midst of a perverted generation. When we see conflict of interpretation we shouldn't say "This is unclear and therefore I don't have to follow it." That is excusing, rather than attempting to understand.

6. There is the substitution of an emotional experience for a volitional act. I get carried away with an "experience" —a new "sensitivity to feeling", a glob of non-directed

emotional vibrations that leave me nowhere. I say, "Oh what a beautiful sermon. Wasn't it eloquent and dramatic," but I avoid the pointed demand for commitment and action.

7. There is the fogging of clear thinking by prejudice, bias, and laziness. I get the human viewpoint or my group's viewpoint confused with the divine, and I'm off on another tangent. Because this truth conflicts with my preconceived ideas, it can't possibly mean that I do thus and so. "And besides, I'd have to give up this habit and attitude to do that, and God doesn't want me to do that yet."

The place to start with application of the Word is with a healthy, immediate response to it, admitting that sinfulness exists within our own hearts and moving in the direction of obedience to Him, with a specific act.

CHAPTER IX.

LEADING THE DISCUSSION

The importance of questions.

Asking questions to help a person discover scriptural principles for himself is not a new technique. Jesus used over one hundred questions in the Gospels. There were many purposes behind the questions of Jesus. One man has said Jesus came not to answer questions but to ask them. Not to settle men's souls, but to provoke them. Jesus used questions to:

1. Secure information. Luke 8:30
2. Express emotion. John 3:10
3. Recall the known. Mark 2:25,26
4. Awaken conscience. Matthew 23:17
5. Elicit faith. Mark 8:29
6. Create a dilemma. Mark 3:4

Jesus often used a leading type of question which suggested the answer He wanted but which allowed the one being questioned to draw his own conclusions. The nature of the leading question is to lead toward a conclusion without forcing acceptance of the answer, or a preconceived idea. For example, in Matthew 5:13 Jesus asked this question on the sermon on the mount. "You are the salt of the earth. But if the salt has lost its taste, how shall its saltiness be restored?" The conclusion is obvious. You need to stay salty to have the effect of salt.

Sometimes He used questions to stop the opposition. He used questions that His foes were unwilling to answer. Compare Matthew 21:25-27, Matthew 22:45, and Luke 14:5,6.

From Jesus' example, you can see that your job as a discussion leader is to help others discover truth for themselves. Therefore, it is necessary for you to cultivate the ability to develop and ask the right questions. These questions become the springboard for discussion in the group. *Do not simply repeat the questions in the lesson,* if it is a question and answer study. Formulate questions which will help the members make new discoveries about what they've studied. Never *tell* when you can *ask.* Be open to answers you *didn't* have in mind. By looking for your own preconceived answer you may miss new insights from God. Questions are valuable because:

1. They help evaluate the group members' understanding, knowledge, and progress in the lesson.
2. They cause the group members to think.
3. They reflect a personal approach which elicits a personal response.
4. They prevent you from becoming the authority figure.
5. They allow the group members to discover truth for themselves.

Robert Lewis Stevenson discerned the value of questions when he said, "You start a question and it's like starting a stone. You sit quietly on top of the hill, and away the stone goes, starting others."

After you have done a Bible study to completion you have in a sense, climbed the mountain. You have discovered, understood, and applied truth. You have attained a sort of satisfaction having walked through the passage of scripture to your destination.

Now that you are on top of a hill, you look down at others who want to climb it. The tendency as a discussion group leader is to throw out all the pearls that you have found along the way. If you do this, you stifle study and quench inquiry especially when you become impatient with others when they don't seem to grasp quickly what you saw.

It is possible to get so bound up in meeting a time limit, trying to cover too much material or waiting impatiently while another stumbles around, that you forget that the purpose of a discussion is to help *others* learn to dig from the Word, and develop *their* relationship to Christ. Your refusal to *listen* or take the time to help them "see" and "understand" what is there, may cool their curiosity to desire more from His Word. Remember, we teach people, not lessons. "People enjoy climbing mountains, but only the feeble enjoy being carried up."

The real key to asking questions is your genuine concern and interest in people. Genuine questioning conveys the attitude that you are truly interested in what people have to say. You cannot successfully fake genuine concern. Neither can you conceal a lack of concern. True dialogue begins when people genuinely want to share in another person's thoughts. If you are really interested in what the other person feels and thinks, you will never be ineffective in asking questions.

It's true that there is an art in asking questions. But anyone who wants to, can learn a lot about the knowledge, skills, and techniques in asking good questions.

There are basically three avenues of questioning in a group discussion. These avenues parallel the three parts of Bible study. These questions are LEADING, GUIDING, AND APPLICATION. These correlate with the parts of Bible study—DISCOVER, UNDERSTANDING, and APPLICATION.

1. LEADING QUESTIONS.

Leading questions are to initiate meaningful discussion of a section or division of the study. The questions you use to start a discussion should be carefully selected. The questions will determine to a large extent both the direction of the discussion and the type of response you will receive. Leading questions are aimed at discovery. You should have two or three carefully prepared in advance for each section of the study, in case one of them or two of them don't really get the discussion started. Some helpful beginning questions could be:

"What have you discovered about _____?"
or,
"What new insights have you seen concerning _____?"
or,
"How does your discovery in this area relate to any other portion of the scripture?"

Leading questions must be simple, relevant, and short. Avoid using "and," "or," "but," in your leading questions as this introduces a second question. Some other general examples of leading questions are,

"What concept in this section was of uppermost importance to you?"

"Would you describe what you studied from this section?"

"What impressed you most from this section?"

2. GUIDING QUESTIONS.

The purpose of guiding questions is to reveal "What does this section mean?" It is aimed at understanding. It is difficult to fully prepare guiding questions in advance because each discussion will determine its own course. However, it is helpful to have a few ideas in mind, prior to the discussion. Your own preparation of the lesson will help you in this.

Each paragraph or division of the lesson should be summarized before the application question is asked. It will be helpful to keep short notes on what was contributed during that part of the discussion in order to be able to summarize it. Your summary might go like this: "It seems that what we have said is, _____". Summarization should clarify, analyze and arrange logically, or structure the chief points in that phase of discussion. One of the keys to learning is to organize, structure, or synthesize the truths discovered. Some examples of guiding questions could be:

"What does that mean?"
"Can you illustrate that?"
"Can you give us an example, preferably from your own experience?"
"How do you relate that to our discussion today?"
"Does someone else have an idea on that?"
"Is there any scripture to help us on that point?"
Some key words to remember in guiding questions are: feel, think, mean, respond.

3. APPLICATION QUESTIONS.

The purpose of application questions is to help each individual determine what he thinks God wants him to do as the result of the study. "What does God want you to do about it?" These questions should draw specific acts or attitudes which the passage being studied implied or commanded. No study is complete without bringing attention to what should be done as the result of what has been studied. These questions will be asked at the end of each section. They should *not* be saved until the end of discussion time. Application should be emphasized throughout the discussion.

A realistic evaluation of your questions can be done by asking the following questions about your questions.

(1) To whom is the question directed?
(2) What is the underlying purpose of the question?
(3) What answer does the question expect or suggest?
(4) How personally are the hearers involved by the question?
(5) What degree of urgency does the question suggest? The more we think about and evaluate the questions we ask, the greater will be our usefulness as a leader and chairman of the group.

Let us remember at the same time that spiritual truths and spiritual gifts are spiritually discerned[16] and that the Lord longs to give us the wisdom from above that we need so much.

"If any of you lack wisdom, let him ask of God, that giveth to all men liberally, and upbraideth not; and it shall be given him."[17]

1. *To whom is the question directed?*
   a. To oneself   —rhetorical
      Avoid rhetorical questions; they usually kill discussion at once.
   b. To one member of the group.   —direct
      Beware of direct questions; the person asked may have nothing relevant to say.
   c. To the one who asked the previous question. —reverse
   d. To the group, other than the previous questioner.
                                                —relay
   e. To the group as a whole   —general
      Normally use general and relay questions; they stimulate the group most.

2. *What is the underlying purpose to the question?*
   Is it to accumulate facts, to define, to clarify, to explain, to compare, to contrast, to develop, to relate, to bring the group back to the subject, to change direction, to involve, to arrive at conclusions, to summarize findings, or to stimulate applications?

---

16 I Corinthians 2:12-14
17 James 1:5

3. What Answer Does the question expect or suggest?

TYPE OF QUESTION	EXAMPLES	ANSWER	VALUE AS GUIDING QUESTION IN LEADING DISCUSSION
a. Loaded	Of course you all agree, don't you? Surely you don't think that, do you? (A question where you have preconceived answer and will accept nothing else)	Yes No	None—it neither stimulates thought nor discussion None—it is clear to all that you've an exact answer in mind. Instead of stimulating discussion, you've started a mind-reading competition. It would be much better to ask: "What are some great truths in this chapter?" Then it becomes an open question.
b. Limiting	What are the three great truths in this chapter? Do you agree with that?	What the group thinks you think. Yes or no.	Some—it insists on a decision. But it must be followed by an open or wide-open question if you want to stimulate further discussion.
c. Open	Who is this all about? Where did this happen? When was this? Why was it? What was the outcome? How can anyone benefit?	People Places Times Reasons Results Conditions	Much—it stimulates discovery, understanding or application according to how you word it. The KEY WORDS are: Who, where, when, why, what, how.
d. Wide-open	What do others think? What does anyone think about that? What does anyone else think?	Any relevant thoughts.	Very much—it stimulates maximum thought discussion. It is best used after an open question has been answered.

4. *How are the hearers involved personally by the question?*

   a. What should other people do
      about this?   —not at all

   b. What should Twentieth
      Century man do about this? —very little

   c. What should unbelievers do —only if the hearers are
      about this? believers?   of the group named.

   d. What should you do about —all except the ques-
      this?   tioner.

   e. What should we do about —all, including the
      this?   questioner.

   f. What will you do about this? —all, fully committed,
                              except the questioner.

   g. What shall we do about this? —all fully committed,
                              including the ques-
                              tioner.

Notice how Jesus Christ helps His disciples to think first objectively (without being personally involved) and only then subjectively (being personally involved) about so important a matter as who He is (Mark 8:27-29, NEB).

Verse 27—"Who do men say I am?"

Verse 29—"Who do you say I am?"

5. *What degree of urgency does the question suggest?*

   a. What could we have done about this? —none

   b. What could we do about this?
      What can we do about this?   —vague

   c. What shall we do about this?
      What should we do about this?   —urgent

   d. What should we do about this, as
      soon as possible?   —most urgent

   e. What should we do about this, when-
      ever possible?   —recurring

There are three criteria for good questions.

(1) Good questions are   **CLEAR**

(2) Good questions are   **RELEVANT**

(3) Good questions   **GET RESPONSE**

1. CLARITY

Does it ask for observations and facts rather than opinions and feelings? Can it be easily remembered and understood? Does it avoid complicated wording?

2. RELEVANCE.

Can it be answered from two or three of the truths in the section of our study? What is the underlying purpose of the question? Does it focus attention on the main point? Does it relate to contemporary life?

3. RESPONSE.

Will it stimulate good participation and discussion? Does it give more than one person opportunity to respond? Does it draw from their personal preparation?

Learn to avoid the use of these types of questions:

GUESSING QUESTIONS which require chance answers. Would make no difference. "Guess which question has the most answers?"

PUMPING QUESTIONS which try to squeeze the right answer from the group members. "What does this mean?" "Okay, what does this mean?" "Okay, what does this mean?"

FACT QUESTIONS which only require knowledge of facts, and generalizations. "What did Jesus do when He went to the temple?"

DIGRESSIONARY QUESTIONS which lead the group astray and off on to tangents. "Concerning the authority of the Bible, what does the Koran have to say?"

DOUBLE-ANSWER QUESTIONS which require two different answers—really, two different questions. "What does this verse say, and what about the verse in the next chapter?"

OBVIOUS ANSWER QUESTIONS which require no thinking or very little. "How many members are in the Trinity?"

QUESTIONS WITH INVOLVED WORDING which are too complicated and complex to answer or understand. "Seeing the 60 different items in chapter two, how many complex and complete sentences can you construct using just a word or two from each verse?"

TOO-DIFFICULT-TO-ANSWER-QUESTIONS which require thinking or facts beyond the aptitude or ability of the reader. "How many camels can get through the eye of a needle?"

QUESTIONS IN A HAP-HAZARD SEQUENCE which have no order or method in the questions. "Who finished the assignment?" "Who would like to begin in prayer?" "Did you understand the chapter?"

Francis Bacon said,
    "A skilled question is the half of knowledge."

CHAPTER X.

SHARING RESPONSIBILITIES

One of the finest opportunities for training others is in the choosing of an assistant who could take your place when you're gone, and eventually start another group. In choosing an assistant, look for the person who will:

1. Pray with you for the group on a regular basis.

2. Help you lead the group more effectively by going over the evaluation after the discussion time.

3. Discuss with you what happened in the discussion. Why it happened and how to improve. He will often be able to see more clearly what happened in the group because he is not under the pressure of asking questions, redirecting questions, and answering questions.

4. Learn how to lead a group himself, so that if you have to be absent he can take the responsibility of leadership.

5. Be prepared to start and lead another group. You should meet with your assistant 10 or 15 minutes before the study and then stay with him 10 to 30 minutes after the study in evaluation.

CHAPTER XI.

HOW TO MAKE THE DISCUSSION MORE INTERESTING

As the old saying goes, "There is more than one way to skin a cat." The same is true in leading a discussion group. There is a sense in which "variety is the spice of life." Don't get in a discussion rut. Try some new approaches. You may be surprised how positive the response will be. Employing audio-visual aids is one way to be a creative leader. The ability to learn and retain knowledge is increased when audio-visual aids are used.

Science has proven that over 70% of our mental impact is made through the eyes. The "eyes have it!" So here are some helpful hints in utilizing visual and audio aids. Try a few before you say "They won't help me!"

Why are visual aids so important to Bible study? They accentuate and strengthen learning in at least eight ways:

1. They catch the students' interest. They get attention, surface needs and curiosity, and orient them to the subject at hand.

2. They contribute to the depth and variety in learning. They offer an alternate to just writing, talking, and listening.

3. They clarify words and concepts. They visualize the verbal, and translate observation and interpretation to communication.

4. They stimulate thought and imagination. They sensitize and personalize objective facts into subjective feelings.

5. They aid logic and reasoning. They allow a viewing of the process, sequence and organization of ideas and concepts.

6. They make learning more permanent. They project upon the mind's eye images and pictures that are permanently etched. They are pass-on-able!

7. They help students assimilate information. They make remembering and learning easy and fun by giving a package construction to study.

8. They aid in personal growth. They emphasize the problems and processes and not the product of growth, showing the relationship of study, time and evaluation.

What are some visual aids that can be used?

1. Slide projector—2x2 slides can be organized into short teaching segments. Make your own slides by taking your own pictures and telling your story with them.

2. Overhead projector—Very useful with your own creative transparencies. They are transferable and useful in small groups. Everybody in the group can use it, adding to your transparency or creating their own.

3. Opaque projector—Although very expensive, it is useful when you want to use material on a screen from a book or picture.

4. Filmstrip projector—Many film strips can be ordered from your local library or denominational Christian education publishers.

How can visual aids be developed for Bible discussion? Here are some tips:

Watch for new ideas. Openness to new ideas, thinking and viewpoints is a key to finding visual aids. You will find visual aids in everyday items. Learn to carry paper and a pencil with you to jot ideas down.

Learn to think creatively. Look for new ways to use familiar aids. Creativity is the ability to view the usual as unusual and the unusual as usual.

Create your own teaching tools. Make your own charts, pictures, cartoons, flash cards, posters, puppets, objects, models, maps, slides, films to illustrate specific lessons.

Visit your local library, church media department or book-store. You may stumble across a book, pamphlet, or article that jogs your thinking, and stimulates a creative thought for a visual aid.

Write publishers and producers for listing of visual aids. Ask for catalouges, listings of films, filmstrips, slides, pictures, object lessons, overhead transparencies, etc.

Check with public school teachers and friends for ideas. One of your greatest sources of ideas is the imagination and thoughts of a friend who is involved in the teaching profession. Some of your best ideas will come from a "brainstorming session" with a few people who want to think along with you.

Visual Helps

1. Pictures—start a file of pictures of things you can use to illustrate material in discussion groups.

2. Exhibits—make a display of useful evangelistic tools or helpful study books and literature.

3. Objects—use common things, like a marble in the hand to show how the Lord has the world in His hand.

4. Specimens—sharing artifacts, a grain of mustard seed, a wheat germ, a grapevine can make a dull conversation more interesting.

5. Charts—chart the course of Paul through Asia Minor, Macedonia, and Africa, and make his travels come alive.

6. Graphs—have the group make a graph of their Christian growth or to show the rise and fall of King David, etc.

7. Maps—a good map of the Bible lands make history and narrative material understandable.

8. Figures—draw figures, sketches, stick-figures to show the action and movement of Bible personalities.

9. Diagrams—a drawing of King Solomon's temple, Jerusalem, or Noah's ark helps communicate size, thought and feeling.

10. Cartoons—add a little humor to otherwise dry material.

11. Posters—great to throw up before a group to communicate ideas, events and attitudes.

12. Chalk boards—every discussion group leader should have one of these on which to write. A newsprint pad serves the same purpose. Both are ideal for writing outlines, sketches, and diagrams.

13. Newspaper and magazines—these are great to draw from for ideas, pictures, and articles.

14. Games—these are fun to play and can be organized around some Biblical principle.

15. Field trips—a trip out to see something of interest or to get involved personally in practicing a newly learned skill can really meet needs. You might take your group on door-to-door evangelism.

16. Dramatization—this fits into the category of role-playing and can be effective in communicating emotions and feeling.

17. Role-playing—taking the part of an angry Herod can add a new dimension to Bible study since you are walking in the shoes of another.

18. Handouts—WHY HANDOUTS ARE IMPORTANT IN BIBLE DISCUSSION:

    They convey large amounts of information for group members to see.

    They leave time for the group to interact and work.

    They are useful in summarizing a session and pointing out key concepts.

    They help communicate a written form, such as "How to Write a Lesson Plan" or "How to Prepare a Testimony."

    They facilitate note-taking and encourage group members to write things down.

Audio Aids

1. Tape recorders, cassette recorders.

2. Phonographs, stereos—sometimes you will find a portion of a record that you will want to play.

3. Radio—you might schedule a Bible discussion during a radio program that corresponds with your topic.

4. Telephone—you can use a telephone in a discussion on prayer, comparing it with our conversation with the Lord.

Audio visual aids offer a variety of opportunities. Try it, you'll like it! The other group members will catch on quickly, and will be adding their own to your accumulation of teaching techniques and tools.

CHAPTER XII.

HANDLING PROBLEMS

In every discussion group you will run into problems. These problems, or obstacles can turn into opportunities with proper handling. Here are some suggestions to help you solve these problems:

How to draw everyone in: Your role as leader is one of a guide, not a teacher. Beware of dominating situations, or appearing to be the final authority on questions that arise. Keep a mental note of those who have not been contributing and direct some questions to them. Be sure the questions are easy so that they are not embarrassed. If necessary, call the group members by name, to help them participate. Leave enough time for them to answer.

How to control the talkative. This is a difficult task. You can call for a contribution from others by asking "What do others think?" or, refer questions specifically to other people. If this doesn't work you may have to have a private conversation with the talker explaining the necessity of group participation and getting that person to help you draw others out.

How to get back on the track. Look upon tangent issues as possible fish bones you may put aside in order to get at the meat. A recognition of the situation generally helps. "This is interesting. However, we have left our topic. Perhaps we could discuss this further after the group has completed its discussion." Or you might suggest that the question be tabled until you complete the idea being discussed. But if you do this don't fake it but actually go back to the question and handle it if they want to.

How to handle wrong answers. Never contradict a person flatly and tell him he is wrong. You might want to direct the same question to someone else in the group. For example, "Okay, what do others think?" or, "Has anyone some scripture which may help us here?" or, "What does someone else have to say about this?"

How to handle silence. Don't be afraid of pauses. Don't try to fill in verbal voids. Give people time to think. The silence may do more good than the discussion has done. The silent times may be uncomfortable times but they are productive.

How to answer questions. Don't ever be afraid of saying "I don't know." You may not know the answers, so don't try to fake one. You don't always have to have the answer but you can tell them that you can find out and discuss it with them later. Someone else in the group may have the answer.

How to cover the lesson. Make a simple lesson plan so you won't get bogged down in the details.

How to handle controversial subjects. When a group faces a serious quest for truth, there is a fear that fellowship may be broken. There is a temptation to skirt the difficult issues of life and to rely on superficial answers. The best way to handle these when they come up is to see what the Word of God has to say and rest the verdict on principles or commands in the Bible which apply to the situation. God's Word is the ultimate authority.

How to spark a lethargic group. Generally, the group will respond to your attitude. Pray for enthusiasm and respond enthusiastically. If you want them to be a little enthusiastic, then you may have to be overly enthusiastic.

How to draw out applications. First, make good, solid applications to your own life from the portion being studied and be willing to share it with them. Then learn to ask effective application questions like, "What does it mean to you?" or, "Is there anything that you can do about this today?"

CHAPTER XIII.

ROLES IN THE GROUP

Dr. Howard Hendricks introduces some amusing but informative characteristics on the roles that people play in a group situation. You'll find yourself identifying with some of these brief character sketches.

Each member of the group is faced with the right and the responsibility of being a mature participant. To accomplish this he must apply himself to the task of being an effective group member, constantly evaluating himself and his relationships with others.

CHARACTERISTICS OF IMMATURITY

Onlooker— Content to be a silent spectator. Nods, smiles and frowns. Other than this, he is a passenger instead of a crew member.

Monopolizer— Brother Chatty. Rambles roughshod over the rest of the conversation with his verbal dexterity. Tenaciously clings to his right to say what he thinks—sometimes without thinking.

Belittler— This is Mr. Gloom. He takes the dim view. Minimizes the contributions of others. Usually has three good reasons why "it will never work."

Wisecracker— Feels called to a ministry of humor. Mr. Cheerio spends his time and talent as the group play-boy. Indifferent to the subject at hand, he is always ready with the clever remark.

Manipulator— Brother Ulterior knows the correct approach to the problem, obviously. He manipulates the proceedings so his plan will be adopted.

Hitchhiker— He has never had an original thought in his life. Unwilling to commit himself. Sits on the sidelines until the decision has jelled, then jumps on the bandwagon.

Pleader— Chronically afflicted with obsessions. Always pleading for some cause or for certain actions. Feels led to share this burden frequently. One-track mind.

Sulker— Born in the objective case and lives in the kickative mood. The group won't accept his worthy contributions so he sulks.

CHARACTERISTICS OF MATURITY

Proposer— Initiates ideas and action. Keeps things moving.

Encourager— Brings others into the discussion. Encourages others to contribute. Emphasizes the value of their suggestions and comments. Stimulates others to greater activity by approval and recognition.

Clarifier— The one who has the facility to step in when confusion, chaos and conflict dominate. He defines the problem concisely. He points out the issues clearly.

Analyzer— Examines the issues closely. Weighs the suggestions carefully. Never accepts anything without first "thinking it through."

Explorer— Always moving in to new and different areas. Probing relentlessly. Never satisfied with the obvious or the traditional.

Mediator— Facilitates agreement or harmony between members; especially those who are making phrases at each other. Seeks to find mediating solutions acceptable to all.

Synthesizer— Is able to put the pieces together. Brings the different parts of the solution or plan together and synthesizes them.

Programmer— The one who is ready with the ways and means to put the proposal into effect. Adept at organization. Moves in the realm of action.

One way to use this material is to read this section to your discussion group, and then have them react and respond to the various roles in the group. You may want them to privately evaluate their role in the group and then publicly discuss it at the next meeting. This type of evaluation helps the group members see themselves for what they really are. It gives each member an appreciation for the other members in the group. The humorous way the above captions are written helps objectify the personal involvement of each member in the group.

CHAPTER XIV.

EVALUATION

It is always good for us to have some form of checkup period. The following questions will help you evaluate your leadership of the discussion group.

LEADER'S PRIVATE EVALUATION

1. Leader's Preparation
   a. Do you consider yourself to have adequately prepared? If not, what was needed?

   b. Did you personalize the group? What did you do with tension? How did you react?

   c. Did you go too deep for the group's ability? Were you too shallow?

   d. How was your eye contact? Your seating position? Your gestures? Voice tone? Mannerisms?

   e. Did you listen? Were you sensitive to group member's needs?

   f. How well did you use illustrations? Visual Aids? Humor?

2. Leader's Planning.

   a. Did you arrive at a useful outline for the discussion, including objectives, introductions, questions, conclusions, etc.?

   b. Did you follow the plan closely? Why or why not?

   c. How should you have introduced and concluded the discussion?

   d. Was the purpose of the discussion clearly grasped by everyone?

   e. Did you plan any illustrations, visual aids or humor?

   f. What did you learn that you could include in future planning?

3. Group Procedures.

   a. Did you guide the discussion with questions? Did you lead or were you led?

   b. Was sufficient relevant information presented to provide a basis for discussion?

   c. Was the desired result of each main question realized? If not, why not?

   d. Was the information carefully observed, interpreted, correlated, and applied?

   e. Did you keep to the subject? Was the material covered? Why not, if not?

   f. What procedures could be eliminated and not affect performance? What new procedures would stimulate the group?

4. Group Participation

   a. Did everyone expected come to the group discussion? If not, why not?

   b. Did everyone in the group take part? (Rank the members in order of how much they talked.)

   c. Were there any tangents? How did they occur? How could they have been avoided or best answered?

   d. Did anyone ever answer or question the group? Did any group member question another group member? Who? How many times?

   e. Was each person stimulated to contribute his best? If not, what could you have done to accomplish this?

   f. Did you notice any members who continuously performed certain functions or played such roles as "harmonizers," "initiators," or "obstructionist"?

5. Group Personalization

   a. Were attitudes of cooperation and permissiveness generally evident?

b. Did the others listen to each other?

c. Was the atmosphere a healthy balance of enthusiasm and relaxed participation?

d. How well do the members know each other?

e. Was each person stimulated to contribute his best? If not, what could you have done to accomplish this?

6. Group Product

a. Were the solutions and conclusions practical and desirable?

b. To what extent was the original objective accomplished?

c. If personal applications were read or shared, were they specific and practical?

d. Have any thinking patterns been changed? Whose? In what way?

From the member's point of view, they each should be able to answer affirmatively to the following five statements.

I have experienced a good discussion session when:

1. I feel that the leader took me right into the subject and not around it.

2. I feel we interacted with the subject itself and not with the personal opinions of the leader.

3. I feel that I now have a better understanding of the truth than before I came to the discussion group.

4. I feel that the time was basically spent in meanings and not in a confusion of religious rules and generalities.

5. I feel challenged, comforted, encouraged and practically instructed.

For further help in evaluating their own behavior, you may want to give them the following 12 questions to answer privately, and then later discuss their feelings as a group. Or you may want to get together with each one personally and discuss the answers. The purpose of these 12 questions is to surface some needs and feelings so that the group can continue to experience spiritual health.

QUESTIONS FOR MEMBER'S PRIVATE EVALUATION

1. What was the most exciting thing you learned this week?

2. What two ways would you improve this discussion group?

3. Do you know the group's objectives?

4. Are you as an individual receiving help in applying the principles learned in the weekly Bible discussion?

5. Do you feel like a member of the discussion group?

6. When you are absent from a weekly discussion, are you missed?

7. Do you have a group of Christian friends with whom you can share the doubts you are ashamed of or embarrased about?

8. If you feel lonely, how effectively are the other group members helping you to feel accepted and needed?

9. Is anyone helping you to control yourself in areas where you know you are irresponsible or unconcerned?

10. In what ways are you learning what your gifts are, and what your ministry is to the Body of Christ?

11. Do you feel inside that other members of the group care whether you sink or swim spiritually?